T0323916

Cambridge Elements

Elements in Translation and Interpreting
edited by
Kirsten Malmkjær
University of Leicester

RESEARCHING AND MODELLING THE TRANSLATION PROCESS

Muhammad M. M. Abdel Latif
Cairo University

Shaftesbury Road, Cambridge CB2 8EA, United Kingdom

One Liberty Plaza, 20th Floor, New York, NY 10006, USA

477 Williamstown Road, Port Melbourne, VIC 3207, Australia

314–321, 3rd Floor, Plot 3, Splendor Forum, Jasola District Centre,
New Delhi – 110025, India

103 Penang Road, #05–06/07, Visioncrest Commercial, Singapore 238467

Cambridge University Press is part of Cambridge University Press & Assessment,
a department of the University of Cambridge.

We share the University's mission to contribute to society through the pursuit of
education, learning and research at the highest international levels of excellence.

www.cambridge.org
Information on this title: www.cambridge.org/9781009532891

DOI: 10.1017/9781009338035

When citing this work, please include a reference to the DOI 10.1017/9781009338035

First published 2024

A catalogue record for this publication is available from the British Library

ISBN 978-1-009-53289-1 Hardback
ISBN 978-1-009-33802-8 Paperback
ISSN 2633-6480 (online)
ISSN 2633-6472 (print)

Cambridge University Press & Assessment has no responsibility for the persistence
or accuracy of URLs for external or third-party internet websites referred to in this
publication and does not guarantee that any content on such websites is, or will
remain, accurate or appropriate.

Researching and Modelling the Translation Process

Elements in Translation and Interpreting

DOI: 10.1017/9781009338035
First published online: November 2024

Muhammad M. M. Abdel Latif
Faculty of Graduate Studies of Education, Cairo University

Author for correspondence: Muhammad M. M. Abdel Latif,
mmmabd@cu.edu.eg

Abstract: Translation process research is almost four decades old. Translator cognition is one of the most complex translation research areas to study. This complexity stems mainly from the difficulties involved in collecting and analyzing translation process data. This work reviews and discusses the developments in translation process research. Specifically, it highlights the key terms in translation process research, its data sources, the developments this area has witnessed in four decades, and the efforts made in modelling the translation process so far. The work also proposes a translation process model which shows the central role monitoring plays in managing other translation subprocesses and evaluating the information being processed. Based on the issues reviewed and discussed, it is concluded that translation process research is still maturing. Making further developments in this translation research area requires addressing some contextual and methodological gaps, and investigating particular neglected research dimensions.

Keywords: translation process, translator cognition, translation strategies, translation problem-solving, translation process models

ISBNs: 9781009532891 (HB), 9781009338028 (PB), 9781009338035 (OC)
ISSNs: 2633-6480 (online), 2633-6472 (print)

Contents

1 Introduction

Translation process research is an area concerned with investigating and understanding translators' cognitive processes and what is involved in the act of translating a text. Early research on translator cognition was published during the second half of the 1980s. Before that time, very few theoretical works highlighted the cognitive activities in translation. For example, in Levý's (1967) work on decision-making processes in translation, translators' cognitive decisions are described as guidelines directing their final choice from competing alternatives. The translation process works published during the 1980s include the ones reported by Dechert and Sandrock (1986), Gerloff (1986, 1987, 1988), Königs (1986, 1987), Krings (1986, 1987, 1988), Jääskeläinen (1987, 1989), Tirkkonen-Condit (1987, 1989), and Séguinot (1989). These early translation process studies were specifically influenced by the widespread use of the think-aloud method in cognitive psychology research at that time (e.g., Ericsson & Simon 1980) and by the seminal think-aloud protocol writing process studies published in the late 1970s and early 1980s (e.g., Flower & Hayes 1977, 1980; Perl 1979).

Several terms have been used interchangeably with 'translation process' research. These include 'translator cognition', 'translation cognition' and 'process-oriented translation' research, and 'cognitive translation studies' (see, e.g., Alves & Jakobsen 2021; Jääskeläinen 1999; Xiao & Halverson 2021). 'Cognitive translatology' is another relevant term that was first used by Muñoz Martín (2009, 2010a; 2010b) who defines it as 'a science of translation and cognition' (Muñoz Martín 2010a, p. 169). Of all these terms, 'translation process research' is perhaps the most commonly used in referring to the area. That is why it is the main term the current work depends on, though readers will note the terms 'translator cognition' and 'translation cognition' are sometimes used interchangeably with it.

Translation process research is characterized by the complexity of its data collection and analysis. Alves and Hurtado Albir (2017) state that the complexity of the translation process can be ascribed to the following features: the multi-directional and non-linear or recursive nature of its components, the role of processing units such as the translator's short- and long-term memories, and the need to coordinate cognitive strategies and the use of external resources. Complexity also concerns translation process data collection and analysis. This complexity is evident, for instance, in Hurtado Albir and Alves's (2009) description of the translation process data analysis:

> The analysis of the translation process entails a great deal of complexity. It is constrained by intrinsic difficulties inherent in studies which aim at tapping into any kind of cognitive processing: it is not amenable to direct observation.

Furthermore, the difficulties related to the investigation of the translation process are magnified by the different phases through which the process unfolds and by the complexity of the interwoven abilities and forms of specialized knowledge which play an integral part in it. (Hurtado Albir & Alves 2009, p. 54)

With these complexities, some researchers label translators' mental processes as the 'black box' (e.g., Krings 1988; Shreve & Koby 1997).

For several reasons, translator cognition is a research area of utmost importance. Some models (e.g., Neubert 1997; PACTE 2000) conceptualize translator competence as made up of a number of components, one of which is the strategic competence encompassing the ability to solve cognitive translation problems and to use translation strategies effectively. According to Lörscher (1992), researching translator cognition can help us understand the dynamics of the translation process, gain insights into language processing and cognitive acts in language use, and identify successful translation strategies. Pedagogically speaking, translation process studies represent one of the six areas of translator education research as represented in Figure 1 which is drawn from Abdel Latif's (2018, 2020) typology. In the figure, the first two areas (translator training experimentation and translation learning and teaching practices research) are directly related to translator education as they deal with the innovative and reliable techniques in translation training and their effectiveness, and with stakeholders' needs, expectations, and evaluation of the training provided. On the other hand, translation process research, along with the other three areas, is indirectly related to translator education. Specifically, it can inform us about translators' process performance difficulties and the types of cognitive strategies used by successful translators. In light of the views of both Lörscher

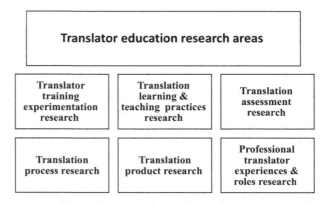

Figure 1 The six areas of translator education research (drawn from Abdel Latif's typology 2018, 2020).

(1992) and Muñoz Martín (2010a), it is generally concluded that translation process research can enrich translators' training by improving their process performance and the quality of their translations, and teaching novice translators the strategies used by proficient translators.

Since its beginning as a field of inquiry, translation process research has witnessed major methodological and research developments. Though many volumes and reviews have been published on these developments (e.g., Alves & Jakobsen 2021; Schwieter & Ferreira 2017; Shreve & Angelone 2010), there is still room for tackling them from a different angle. In this Element, the author will specifically highlight the following main issues: (a) key terms in translation process research; (b) data collection and analysis methods in translation process research; (c) the key issues researched so far in translation process studies; and (d) the developments in translation process modelling.

2 Defining Key Terms

To avoid any potential terminological confusion, it is important to define and describe the nature of some key terms in translation process research. Specifically, we need to distinguish between the terms 'translation process', 'translation processes/sub-processes', and 'translation strategies'. Understanding these terms will also be helpful in discussing the issues covered in the following sections.

The term 'translation process' is generally used to refer to the cognitive strategies and behaviours involved in the act of translating a source text into a target text. However, researchers have defined this term differently. According to Hvelplund (2011), there are two different notions of the translation process: (a) the narrower cognitive notion which views it as a set of mental and problem-solving operations used in converting a text from one language to another; and (b) the broader notion which defines the translation process more comprehensively by viewing it as encompassing all the mental and non-mental actions and behaviours leading eventually to translating a source text into a target one. The following two definitions can be regarded as representative of the first notion:

- Translation is 'a complex cognitive process which has an interactive and non-linear nature, encompasses controlled and uncontrolled processes, and requires processes of problem-solving, decision-making and the use of strategies and tactics' (Alves & Hurtado Albir 2010, p. 28).
- 'A translation product is the end result of the activation of a particular kind of cognitive information-processing system [that] engages all the underlying subsystems of the brain's cognitive architecture. Translation is an emergent process that requires executive control, attention, and working and long-term memory systems to work together' (Diamond & Shreve 2017, pp. 479–480).

Meanwhile, the following definition is an example of the second notion as it views the translation process as:

- 'Everything that happens from the moment the translator starts working on the source text until he finishes the target text. It is all encompassing, from every pencil movement and keystroke, to dictionary use, the use of the internet and the entire thought process that is involved in solving a problem or making a correction – in short everything a translator must do to transform the source text to the target text' (Hansen 2003, p. 26).

In this Element, the second cognitive notion of the translation process is adopted; that is, defining it as an all-encompassing process. Arguably, a more reliable cognitive conceptualization of the whole translation process or any of its components should consider all that it includes. Based on their review of cognitive models of translation, Hurtado Albir and Alves (2009) refer to the following characteristics of the translation process:

- It has basic phases related to understanding and re-expression.
- It is characterized by using mental information resources stored in the long-term and short-term memories, and external sources such as dictionaries and references.
- It is a non-linear and recursive process.
- It encompasses a mixture of conscious and subconscious or controlled and uncontrolled behaviours.
- It primarily depends on using problem-solving, information retrieval, decision-making, and translation-specific strategies.

In light of the definitions and notions given in this section, translation can be defined from a cognitive perspective as a recursive and interactive process which encompasses using, activating, and coordinating different types of sub-processes, strategies, knowledge, resources, and short- and long-term memory systems to optimally transform a source text into a target text. As noted, this definition of the translation process includes the terms 'translation sub-processes' and 'translation strategies'. The whole translation process encompasses sub-processes such as monitoring, source text representation, target text rehearsing and revising; that is, the term 'sub-processes' means 'translation process components'. Meanwhile, readers will also note in many cases in this work the plural form 'translation processes' is used interchangeably with the terms 'translation sub-processes' and 'translation process components'. In other words, the plural form (i.e., translation processes) refers to the components of the singular form (i.e., the whole translation process).

Translation process components or sub-processes also include 'strategies'. According to Kiraly (1995), translation strategies are minor processes. In translation research, the term 'translation strategies' has two different meanings: textual versus cognitive strategies. Cognitive translation strategies differ from textual translation strategies or 'translation procedures', a comparative stylistic term coined in translation studies by Vinay and Darbelnet (1958) and it refers to formulating lexical, morpho-syntactic, and semantic equivalences in two languages (Bardaji 2009). In this Element, the term 'translation strategies' is used interchangeably with 'cognitive strategies'. In language learner process research, the word 'strategy' is used interchangeably with other terms such as 'behaviours', 'tactics', 'operations', 'actions', and 'steps'.

Researchers have conceptualized translation strategies as mainly mental operations used in performing tasks and they also associate such strategies with solving translation problems or reaching goals (e.g., Kiraly 1995; Lörscher 1991). However, in their task performance, translators use strategies or behaviours such as checking time, self-encouragement (i.e., motivation regulation), circling or underlining a text part as a reminder, transcribing, and textual revising; these strategies are not mental. As explained in in the above paragraphs, the broader approach to researching translator cognition involves looking at all types of strategies, steps, or actions translators use while performing a translation task rather than their mental operations only. In light of this, translation strategies can be defined as the behaviours or steps translators use to complete their tasks, manage task performance, and solve translation problems. Researchers have also talked about the conscious versus unconscious (Lörscher 1991) or controlled versus uncontrolled (automatic) translation process strategies (Kiraly 1995). This has been a controversial issue. While Lörscher (1991) states that a translation strategy is 'a potentially conscious procedure' for solving translation problems (p. 76), research has not decisively differentiated yet between conscious and unconscious translation process strategies.

3 Data Collection and Analysis in Translation Process Research

A number of data sources have been used in previous translation process research. Collectively, these can be classified into three main types: introspective sources, observational sources, and retrospective sources. In the following subsections, these data sources are described and discussed.

3.1 Introspective Data Sources

Methodologically speaking, introspection generally means examining one's thoughts and perceptions. An introspective data source enables us to look at research participants' reports of inner thoughts and emotions. As will be noted in the works cited in the following two subsections, translation process research has made use of two introspective sources: the think-aloud method conducted in individual sessions and the dialogue think-aloud method conducted synchronously with more than one research participant.

3.1.1 The Think-Aloud Method

The think-aloud method was the primary data source early translation process research drew upon (e.g., Gerloff 1986; Jääskeläinen 1989; Königs 1987; Krings 1987). When using this method, researchers ask participant translators to verbalize whatever comes to their minds while performing the translation task; these verbalizations are recorded, and then transcribed and analysed. The translators' recorded verbalizations as well as the translated texts they produce and any notes they write down are labelled 'think-aloud protocols' (Smagorinsky 1994). The analysis of these protocols is mainly based on inferring the translation strategies used while performing the target task. Approaches to analysing translators' strategies in the think-aloud protocol data vary depending on the purpose of the study; see Sun (2011) for some guidelines for analysing translators' think-aloud protocol data.

Ericsson and Simon (1980, 1993) have made a significant contribution to standardizing the use of the think-aloud method in cognitive research. Based on the time interval between performing the cognitive process and verbalizing it, Ericsson and Simon (1980) categorize research participants' verbalized thoughts as either concurrent or retrospective verbalizations. A concurrent verbalization occurs if the participant is synchronously uttering it at the moment of performing a particular cognitive operation, whereas a retrospective verbalization is the outcome of asking the participant to recall the activity performed earlier. Ericsson and Simon (1993) give further descriptions of these verbalizations through classifying them into three levels: (a) Level 1 verbalization: verbalizing one's thoughts without trying to communicate them; (b) Level 2 verbalization: uttering the information held in one's short-term memory without bringing it into the focus of attention; and (c) Level 3 verbalization: verbalizing one's thoughts through linking them to the information processed at a previous time.

Many criticisms have been raised with regard to using the think-aloud method in translation process studies. Smagorinsky (1994), for instance, states that the method does not 'elicit all cognitive activity, and therefore [is] incomplete … [and] conducted under the artificial conditions of time-constrained sessions' (Smagorinsky 1994, p. 4). Li (2004) also points out that there are concerns over the rigor and trustworthiness of think-aloud protocol translation studies as their design leaves much to be desired and their findings can be regarded almost as working hypotheses that need to be tested in further translation research. Other criticisms of the think-aloud method relate to its reactivity and validity. Validity depends on the correspondence between the thoughts verbalized and the actual cognitive operations performed during the task (Green 1998), whereas reactivity means that the think-aloud method may potentially cause changes in participants' cognitive processes during task performance (Leow & Morgan-Short 2004). According to Russo, Johnson, and Stephens (1989), the reactivity of the think-aloud method may be caused by factors such as the additional processing load, auditory feedback or stimuli, and enhanced learning resulting from repeated trials.

The concerns raised by Russo and colleagues have been discussed in translation process studies as well. For example, Jakobsen (2003) found that the think-aloud method caused a delay of about 25 per cent in the translation process and resulted in producing translated text in smaller segments than were produced without think-aloud. Sun, Li, and, Zhou's (2020) study also revealed a negative influence of the think-aloud method on the duration of the translation process, the cognitive effort load in the drafting phase, and the perceived level of translation difficulty. In addition to these translation research-specific findings, some writing studies showed that the think-aloud method slowed writers' composing performance and decreased their fluency and textual syntactic variety (e.g., Yang, Hu, & Zhang 2014).

Think-aloud protocol translation studies have also been criticized for not having an established research paradigm, that is systematic research designs and data analysis approaches. Bernardini (2001) elaborates on this issue as follows:

> [A] major problem with [think-aloud protocol] studies has been the lack of an established research paradigm, resulting in a rather loose treatment of methodological issues (research design, data analysis, research report) and in a host of studies setting their own categorisations in a theoretical void. Most of the research reports we have been concerned with so far describe the research design summarily, present findings in an anecdotal fashion, do not provide any statistical analysis of their data (and sometimes not even the data themselves) and leave central theoretical assumptions unexplained. The reader thus finds it difficult to assess the validity of the results obtained. (p. 251)

Though Bernardini's view was reported more than two decades ago, the lack of an established research paradigm remains in translation process research, largely because there has been a decrease in think-aloud translation studies since the beginning of the millennium (Bernardini 2001; Sun 2011). Noting some hibernation in using the think-aloud method in translation process research, Sun (2011) surveyed the relevant views and research practices of 25 internationally eminent translation researchers with research experience with the method. While 23 survey respondents in Sun's study valued the think-aloud method highly, only seven of them continued to conduct think-aloud translation research. The two main reasons given for the decline of think-aloud translation research were the availability of objective observational methods such as computer keystroke logging and eye-tracking, and the very time-consuming nature of think-aloud translation studies. The last point is true particularly with regard to think-aloud data transcription which involves incorporating the participant's verbalizations, translated text, and written notes (if any) into one protocol and differentiating between what is being verbalized and what is being written, and between what is being read and what is being repeated. For instance, Krings (2001) reported that he transcribed 100 hours of audio-recorded think-aloud data in 1600 hours. The author's own experience in transcribing think-aloud writing process data also confirms this time-consuming concern as it took him about 600 working hours to transcribe a 28-hour audio-recorded think-aloud data set. Though automatic speech recognition software has made verbal data transcription easier, it is still questionable whether this case also applies to the translation process think-aloud data whose transcription requires using a number of transcription conventions representing different types of the translator's verbalizations and written texts.

Despite the above-mentioned criticisms and constraints, the think-aloud method remains a very important data source of the translation process. The method provides researchers not only with insights into translators' mental processes but also with important data about their behavioural and transactional operations (Jääskeläinen 2002). Think-aloud protocols have been a key source for understanding translation cognition. The importance of using think-aloud aloud protocols in translation process research lies also in that they can be the primary data source for modelling translators' processes and strategies. In writing research – which is a very close linguistic research area to translation – most process models have mainly been developed based on think-aloud protocol data (e.g., Abdel Latif 2021; Flower & Hayes 1980). Abdel Latif (2019a) found that compared to retrospective interviews, the think-aloud method helps in gaining far deeper insights into written text production processes, providing much more accurate and detailed data about complex and different text composing strategies. Similar advantages are believed to apply to translation process data if collected using the think-aloud method. Likewise, the insights we can get from the think-aloud protocols about translators' retrieval and monitoring strategies are unobtainable from any other data source (Jakobsen 2017).

While using the think-aloud method in translation process research is on the decline, translation researchers can try to standardize its use instead of completely abandoning it. For example, the reactivity of the method can be overcome by providing participants with adequate training in verbalizing their thoughts. Such training should enable research participants to generate concurrent rather than retrospective verbalizations, and verbalize their thoughts in a way conforming to the Level 1 or Level 2 verbalization procedures proposed by Ericsson and Simon (1993).

A thorny issue in collecting data using the think-aloud method concerns the researcher's visibility in the session. According to Hansen (2005), while the researcher is supposed to be present in the think-aloud session, they should remain invisible. Ericsson and Simon (1993) suggest using reminders to make the participant speak when they stop verbalizing their thoughts, but they recommend that these reminders should have a minimal influence upon participants' processing. Jääskeläinen (1999), who notices that think-aloud participants tend to stop verbalizing their thoughts during high cognitive load moments, states that the researcher's minimal intervention enhances the ecological validity of the experiment, that is, the similarity of the of the participants' translation performance in think-aloud session to real-life tasks. On the other hand, both Hillocks (1986) and Chamot (2001) consider that the researcher's presence in the think-aloud session may negatively influence the participant's task performance and verbalizations. In light of these different views, it is generally recommended that the researcher should not be present in the same place where the participant is completing the language task and verbalizing their thoughts. Instead, the researcher can observe the participant from another room and remind them (through a microphone) to verbalize their thoughts only when needed. It is also recommended that the think-aloud method be administered to as many participants as possible in order to obtain a sufficient number of reliable and valid protocols. This is due to the possibility that not all participants have been able to verbalize their thoughts properly. The time-consuming transcription of the think-aloud translation process can be accelerated by using evolving transcription technologies.

Two main issues need to be taken into account when analysing and reporting think-aloud data. First, many think-aloud translation process studies have compared participants' strategies or behaviours in terms of their raw numbers rather than percentages. This approach may result in misleading results when some participant translators spend more time on the task or are able to verbalize more thoughts than their peers. In writing process research, Rijlaarsdam and van den Berg (1996) argue that analysing the percentages of verbalized composing behaviours is fairer than analysing their raw frequencies as the former method shows the relative contribution of each behaviour to the whole writing process. Roca de Larios and colleagues (1999, 2008) have adopted this analysis approach to neutralise inter-participant variability of thought verbalization and the time spent on the task. We need also to consider the introspective nature of translation process think-aloud data. Given the nature of such data, we generally cannot expect to draw much upon inferential statistics when comparing translators' process strategies. Optimally, we can treat participant translators' think-aloud data as case studies and thus depend more on analysing them qualitatively. Accumulated profiles and evidence gained from think-aloud studies can help us at the end to achieve a breakthrough in describing translator cognition and diagnosing their process problems.

3.1.2 Dialogue Protocols (the Dialogue Think-Aloud Method)

While the issues mentioned in the previous subsection pertain to the think-aloud method when administered in individual sessions – that is, obtaining monologue verbalizations from participant translators, some studies have engaged participants in generating dialogue protocols to obtain think-aloud data from them while performing joint translation tasks. This approach to collecting think-aloud translation process data has been commonly labelled 'dialogue protocols'. Pavlović (2009) also refers to it as 'collaborative translation protocols' and defines these tasks as ones in which two or more research participants work together in translating the same source text and making mutual decisions in solving translation problems. Early translation studies employing the dialogue think-aloud method have been published since the late 1980s but they occurred infrequently (e.g., House 1988; Kussmaul 1997; Schmid 1994). It is also worth noting that some of these few studies have primarily focused on comparing the two methods as data sources (e.g., House 1988; Li & Cheng 2011; Matrat 1992).

The dialogue think-aloud method is viewed as a way of overcoming the concerns raised about the reactivity and validity of the monologue think-aloud method. According to House (1988), this method enables researchers to get richer data as compared to the monologue think-aloud method. Empirically, researchers have found that compared to their monologue think-aloud protocols, participant translators' dialogue protocols show more complex problem-solving processes (House 1988) and include more verbal data due to the more natural verbalization environment it provides (Li & Cheng 2011; Matrat 1992). Besides, research indicates that participant translators have a more positive attitude towards verbalizing their thoughts in collaborative translation tasks than in individual ones (Li & Cheng 2011).

Despite these merits, the dialogue think-aloud method is not without its limitations. For instance, Kussmaul and Tirkkonen-Condit (1995) state that dialogue protocols may not show us a clear picture of collaborative processes because personality traits rather than translation abilities may lead one research participant to take a more leading role than their task collaborators in verbalizing translation problem solutions. To minimize this potential problem, they recommend paying attention to forming translation task completion groups with members of equal psychological and social traits. Kussmaul and Tirkkonen-Condit (1995) also suggest analysing dialogue protocol parts in which participant translators equally take part in translation problem-solving.

Another main limitation of dialogue think-aloud translation process protocols is that they provide us with different data as compared to the data obtained from monologue protocols. According to Jääskeläinen (2000) and Göpferich and Jääskeläinen (2009), the data provided by dialogue protocols do not reflect individual translation processes. Kussmaul and Tirkkonen-Condit (1995) also point out that while researchers try 'to observe what goes on in a translator's mind we are now not observing one mind at work but two or more, and that we record thoughts that would never have occurred to a single translator' (Kussmaul and Tirkkonen-Condit 1995, p. 180). Unlike the dynamics characterizing individual translation processes, the transcribed collaborative think-aloud protocol data and the analysis units Pavlović (2007, 2009) provided clearly show that in this translation task type the meaning is constructed and problems are solved through conversations. Therefore, the dialogue think-aloud method should not be regarded as an alternative data source to its monologue counterpart; it is ideally suitable for collecting data about collaborative or group translation tasks rather than individual ones.

3.2 Observational Data Sources

Observational data sources have been increasingly used in translation process research published since the beginning of the millennium. Increasing use is particularly notable in employing technology-based observation data sources. Conversely, only a few translation process studies have relied upon the researcher's observation.

3.2.1 Technology-Based Observation

Previous translation process studies have made use of the following three technology-based observational data sources: keystroke logging, eye-tracking, and screen recording. Using computer-keystroke logging in translation process research entails observing and analysing participant translators' strategies or behaviours through recording their computer screen activities and their timings, including: keyboard presses, cursor movements, text reading, use of computer-based resources, and pausing between translation acts. The earliest keystroke logging translation process studies occurred at the turn of the century (e.g., Jakobsen 1999; Lauffer 2002).

The real-time computer keystroke logging software commonly used in translation process research is Translog (see Jakobsen 2011; Jakobsen & Schou 1999). Translog provides precise time records of keyboard activities and mouse cursor movements, and saves such activities in a logging file. Thus, it allows researchers to access data about translators' pausing, and text deletions and changes, and to replay these keyboard and mouse activities for later analysis or for stimulating participant translators' retrospective thoughts about their translation processes. According to Jakobsen (2011), the original rationale for developing Translog was to reach a better understanding of the dynamic interaction between the processes involved in translation by supplementing qualitative think-aloud protocols with quantitative behavioural data about the temporal patterns of typing and pausing during the translation process. Another computer keystroke logging software employed in previous translation process research is Proxy which provides researchers with translation process profiles similar to Translog data, and it also enables them to see other computer screens translators use such as dictionary software and search engines (Alves & Hurtado Albir 2010; PACTE 2003, 2005).

Computer-based translation process logged data has been analysed in different ways, depending on the research topic addressed. In most previous studies, pausing has been the main temporal aspect analysed. In these studies, it is noted that logged data has helped researchers to refine what can be regarded as a significant pause. Compare, for instance, Krings' (1986) think-aloud protocol study, in which a significant pause was set at three or more seconds, to Dragsted's (2010) keystroke logging study which depended on a 1-second pause. A main advantage Translog offers is helping translation process researchers examine translators' pausing at 0.01 seconds and to set a pause value of 1–5 seconds (for more details, see Kumpulainen 2015). Researchers have used pausing in computer logged data as an indicator of translators' cognitive processes such as source or target text reading, and problem-solving reflection. They have used pause duration (e.g., short versus long pauses) and location (e.g., pausing between sentence, clause, phrase, word, and word-medial boundaries) as indicators for inferring translators' cognitive processes during each pause type, see for example Kruger (2016) and Muñoz Martín and Cardona Guerra (2019). Previous keystroke logging studies have also analysed the time allocated to each stage or component in the translation process, for example: task execution time, text production time, total pause time, and pause count (e.g., de Lima Fonseca 2019). Other translation process features analysed in previous keystroke logging studies include: text insertions, deletions, return keystrokes, copy/cut-and-paste keystrokes, mouse operations, and resource search, for example, concordance search, Google search, and dictionary search (for more details, see, e.g., Abdel Latif (2020); Bundgaard & Christensen (2016, 2019)).

As a data source, keystroke logging offers researchers some advantages. It is an unobtrusive source for obtaining written text production data, i.e., it does not distract translators' cognitive processes. Replaying the keystroke-recorded writing sessions also allows researchers to understand the problems participants encounter while performing translation tasks. Additionally, real-time computer-based logged data of written text production can be archived and studied by other researchers (Abdel Latif 2008; Levy & Ransdell 1996). It is also a rich source for studying particular aspects of translators' processes such as their pausing and translation activity timing and duration, and the distribution of time and effort allocated to translation activities. Through keystroke logging, we can obtain a detailed overview of the complete and timed sequence of the translation activity and its dimensions such as chunking, pausing and pause distribution, edits and corrections (Jakobsen 2011). Unlike the think-aloud method, real-time computer keystroke logging can be used with translators of different ages and different ability levels.

Despite these merits, relying on computer keystroke logging in translation process research is not without its limitations. Some professional translators may resist taking part in research requiring computer logged data due to safety reasons. In other words, they may not agree to install keystroke logging software on their PCs as it could be regarded spyware (Ehrensberger-Dow 2014). Analysing and interpreting the logged data of the translation process is not an easy process either. According to Jakobsen (2011), it is usually difficult to infer translators' cognitive processes from their pauses in a keystroke record; while translators may pause for source or target text reading, or problem-solving, we may end up with only successfully inferring the strategies the translator engages in just before typing a text chunk. O'Brien (2006a) recommends supplementing pause analysis of the logged data with other data sources. In translation process research, keystroke logging data have frequently been combined with one or more of the following data sources: the think-aloud method, eye-tracking, and computer screen recording.

Eye-tracking is a procedure for recording research participants' eye-movements and fixations on a computer-displayed content in order to gain insights into their cognitive operations. Historically, the use of eye-tracking in studying linguistic information processing originated in the reading area. During the last decades of the twentieth century, linguistic research started to make more use of eye-tracking as a data source, but this research was primarily of a psycholinguistic orientation. In the last two decades, eye-tracking has gained increasing ground in language learning and applied linguistics studies (for more information, see Abdel Latif (2019b)). It was only after 2005 when early eye-tracking translation process studies occurred (e.g., Dragsted & Hansen 2008; Göpferich, Jakobsen, & Mees 2008; O'Brien 2006a, 2006b, 2008, 2009; Pavlović & Jensen 2009). Since that time, eye-tracking has widely become a supplementary data source in translation process studies. It has particularly been combined with computer keystroke logging in many published translation process studies.

The eye-tracking data analysis in translation process research has primarily focused on translators' reading and visual behaviours. For example, Jakobsen (2011) drew upon eye-tracking to identify the target and source text parts translators fixated. Dragsted and Carl (2013) also analysed eye-tracking data in terms of translators' source text reading during the drafting phase, and their looking ahead and looking back during reading (i.e., translators' fixation on the source text word or phrase being translated versus their fixation on what has already been translated, respectively). For more details about methods of analysing translation process eye-tracking data, see Abdel Latif (2019b, 2020), Hvelplund (2014), and O'Brien (2009).

As implied in the above two paragraphs, eye-tracking tools can show us translation process data dimensions obtainable from no other source. It provides a unique window for investigating and understanding written text production processes (Yu, He, & Isaacs 2017). Like keystroke logging, eye-tracking data is also collected in a more natural and less unobtrusive way than when using other sources such as the think-aloud method. Unlike the think-aloud method, eye-tracking data can be collected from translators of different ages and experiences. Despite these merits, eye-tracking has some data collection shortcomings which relate to the eye-tracker used, participant selection, experimental conditions, and data analysis (Alves, Pagano, & da Silva 2009; Hvelplund 2014). Hvelplund (2014) raises some precautions with regard to these issues:

> Eye-tracking data can potentially be misrepresentative of actual cognitive processing if caution is not exercised when collecting it. In terms of the choice of eye-tracker, remote eye-trackers are generally better suited for translation research because they are less invasive than head-mounted and head-supported systems. . . . [T]here is a host of confounding factors that are not necessarily linked to the translator's problem-solving activities during

translation, and they could potentially distort the analyses of the recorded translations . . . including changes in light intensity and the emotional state . . . and the researcher should aim at controlling for these potentially error-inducing factors when collecting the data and also when analysing it. . . . Even if precautions have been taken during data collection, the quality of the eye-tracking data might still be poor and overall not reflect the translator's process. An important step in the analysis phase is, therefore, to discard low-quality data. (Hvelplund 2014, pp. 219–220)

In the above cited part, Hvelplund refers to a number of issues researchers need to consider when selecting eye-trackers, participants, and in experimental conditions and data analysis. In addition to these considerations, translation process researchers need also to avoid eye-tracking jargon when presenting the results of data analysis. This happens, for instance, when data description is more concerned with translators' eye-movements and fixations rather than their cognitive processes. Overall, we still need more fine-grained approaches for presenting eye-tracking data and transforming its jargon into labels describing translators' actual cognitive processes.

As for screen recording, it has been used for supplementing data collected from other sources, particularly keystroke logging, think-aloud protocols, and retrospective interviews. With an appropriate screen recording application downloadable in a computer device, researchers can obtain all on-screen activities the participant has performed during the translation task. Following task completion, the recorded video(s) can be analysed at a later stage or may be played back to stimulate the participant's retrospective thoughts about their translation processes (Angelone 2012). Camtasia[1] has been one of the most commonly used screen recording software in translation process studies.

Computer screen recording provides researchers with ecologically valid and real-time data about translators' processing, and it is a user-friendly and unobtrusive data source (Angelone 2012). In previous studies, screen-recorded data has been used for capturing the translator's use of electronic and online sources, and for identifying their cognitive effort as measured by using processing speed (words per second), and their pause duration which indicates translation problems and problem-solving (Alves & Campos 2009; Angelone 2010a; Christensen 2011). Screen-recorded translation process has also been used for stimulating participants' thoughts about their cognitive processes in retrospective interviews, and as a reflective tool in translation process training. Angelone (2010a), for instance, gave the following brief description of

---

[1] For more information about Camtasia, and how to download and use it, please visit this page: www.techsmith.com/camtasia/.

how to implement computer screen recordings in raising trainees' awareness of effective translation processes:

> Prior to having students engage in self-reflection, it is paramount for trainers to guide them through the process and introduce various focal points, starting with potential problem indicators embedded in the screen recordings. Primary problem indicators include extended pauses in screen activity, instances of information retrieval, and revisions, among others. When analysed empirically by students on a regular basis and across a variety of translation tasks, these are the kinds of phenomena that can yield a more holistic understanding of the nature of problems and problem-solving.

The benefits of using computer screen recordings in translation process training have been confirmed by empirical studies (e.g., Angelone 2019; Pym 2009).

3.2.2 Researcher's Observation

Researcher's observation has occasionally been employed in previous translation process studies to supplement data collected from other sources. The observational notes taken can also be used to stimulate translators' retrospective accounts in post-observation interviews. Researcher's observation normally focuses on the 'physical translation activities that involve task-oriented operations and actions as behavioural, observable action patterns' (Risku 2014, p. 339). The translation process aspects the researcher may observe may include: the time the translator spends on source text reading, source consultation, pausing during the task, and the translator's emotional state as indicated by facial expressions and body language. Researcher's observation should be conducted in a way that will not influence the translator's behaviours. Therefore, researchers need to observe translators from a distance or remotely with a camera. Preparing a checklist of what to observe in the translation task prior to conducting the observational data is important.

Mossop (2000) made a systematic observation of the procedures translators use in their workplace, and combined his observational notes with interviews. In his study report, Mossop provided sample descriptions of the observational notes of two translators. The observational notes of the first translator covered the scanning of the source text, understanding the translation task, consulting sources, marking a part of the translated text so as to get back to it for fixing a particular problem at a later phase of the task, asking the source text author about the intended meaning of a text part, proofreading the target text, and reviewing a printout of the target text to give it a final edit. As for the observational notes of the second translator, these concerned the above-mentioned procedures along with others, such as evaluating one's familiarity with the source text language while scanning it, consulting different types of sources, and reviewing translated text formatting in a printout.

Some previous translation process studies have relied upon video recording for taking observational notes. For example, Lauffer (2002) supplemented her think-aloud data through using a camera for recording the participant translators' facial expressions and body language, and their verbalizations and source consultation behaviours. However, Lauffer noticed that video recording caused the participants to feel that they were in a laboratory rather than in a natural translation workplace setting. On the other hand, Hirvonen and Tiittula (2018) studied team translation processes through multimodal conversation analysis of video-recorded data. In their study report, they included transcriptions from this video to show the translators' negotiation of target text words.

As noted in the examples given in this subsection, researcher's observation may be the easiest method for collecting data about translators' processes. However, it can only inform us about some physical activities in such processes. That is why researcher's observation may often be useful in supplementing other data sources.

3.3 Retrospective Data Sources

Retrospective data sources are employed for assessing research participants' cognitive processes. Their use is based on the assumption that participants can retrieve such processes from the information stored in long-term memory (Ericsson & Simon 1993). One main advantage of using retrospective sources in collecting data about translators' processes is that they do not interfere with the translation process itself; however, the retrospective data retrieved by research participants may be incomplete or inaccurate (Englund Dimitrova & Tiselius 2009). Interviews and questionnaires are the two main retrospective data sources that have been used in previous translation process research.

3.3.1 Retrospective Interviews

With retrospective interviews, researchers try to collect data about cognitive processes stored in participant translators' long-term memory. In previous translation process research, two main types of retrospective interviews have been used: task-specific interviews and non-task-specific ones. Non-task-specific interviews can be used for exploring translators' habitual translation processes and strategies. Thus, they can inform us about the socio-cognitive aspects of translators' processes. This interview type has been used in a limited number of studies. One of these studies was reported by LeBlanc (2013) who interviewed a group of translators about, among other things, the interaction with translation memory systems during text translation and their editing processes. LeBlanc's data showed that translation memory systems have changed the translators' relationship with the text by requiring them to work with translation segments or units rather than the whole text and by making the process of re-organizing the target text (i.e., combining, splitting, and moving sentence parts) more complicated. A few other studies have used retrospective interviews with both task-specific and non-task-specific questions. For example, Bundgaard's (2017) non-task-specific retrospective interview questions revealed important data about translators' cognitive processes when integrating machine translation changes or when machine translation software produces no matches and about the nature of translators' concordance searches.

Task-specific retrospective interviews are normally semi-structured ones – i.e., guided by some key questions – conducted with participant translators after they perform their translation tasks. Translators' task-specific retrospective thoughts are facilitated if the task is short and has been performed recently (Englund Dimitrova & Tiselius 2009). In this interview type, researchers try to stimulate participant translators to retrieve accounts about their translation strategies and processes drawing upon some cues in a data set collected using another source. In previous translation process research, task-specific retrospective interviews have been combined with different cues. For example, Bundgaard and Christensen (2016), Bundgaard (2017), and Bundgaard and Christensen (2019) drew upon screen recording and observational notes to stimulate translators' retrospective thoughts about using machine translation technologies. In the three studies, the participant translators watched parts of screen recordings and were asked some questions about their translation processes. In their study about student translators' justifications for their translation solutions, Vottonen and Kujamäki (2021) followed the same approach. They describe the collection and analysis of their retrospective interview data as follows:

> The translation process was recorded with the screen recording software Camtasia Studio 8. Immediately after the task, participants performed retrospection in which they described their translation process to the researcher with the screen recording as a cue. ... During the retrospections, students could describe their translation process and decision-making freely. During silent moments or clear problems during the translation process, the researcher asked 'what is going on here' or 'what were you thinking at this point', without prompting the use of theoretical concepts. Retrospections were recorded and transcribed. The data was analysed using content-based analysis. We scrutinised the transcriptions simultaneously with the screen recordings, picking out points at which students refer to decision-making and provide some justification for their solutions (rather than, for example, just explaining what they are

doing). ... The use of metalanguage was also considered as a potential signal of verbalised decision-making. The analysis was data-driven: we did not reflect students' justification on any existing categorisation, but different categories arose from the data. (Vottonen & Kujamäki 2021, pp. 312–313)

It is worth noting that Dam-Jensen and Heine (2009) suggest considering research participants' retrospection capacities by getting them to reflect on 15–20 minutes only of the screen recorded content, and also providing them with some guidance for retrieving their translation processes when viewing the visual recorded data.

On the other hand, Hansen (2006) combined retrospective interviews and keystroke logging to help translators retrieve their cognitive processes. With this approach, the participant's translation task performance is recorded using computer keystroke logging, and then the recorded translation session is replayed to the participant who retrieves their translation strategies during particular stages of the task. Hansen specifically differentiates between two types of retrospection: retrospection with replaying keystroke logging data (R+Rp) and retrospection with replaying keystroke logging data and immediate dialogue (R+Rp+ID). Below is Hansen's description of these two retrospective methods:

> Retrospection with replay [i.e., R+Rp] means that [participants] work alone throughout the whole test or experiment. The observer only disturbs them after the translation process is finished in order to save the target text and to establish and start the replay function. After that, [participants] observe the replay of their writing process on the screen and comment on the translation process, problems and problem-solving. The reports are recorded and transcribed. ... For [R+Rp+ID], ... the observer is present during the replay and listens to the retrospection. Immediately after the [participant] stops commenting on his/her translation process, the observer initiates a retrospective dialogue with the [participant] about phenomena like ... behaviour during the process, individual problems, problem-solving, errors and any other issues that might seem to be relevant. (p. 6)

It is worth mentioning that the second type of retrospection (i.e., R+Rp+ID) is far more common in translation process research and in language learner process studies than the former type (i.e., R+Rp).

3.3.2 Self-report Instruments: Questionnaires and Process Logs

Self-report instruments (i.e., questionnaires and process logs) are used to explore the strategies respondents use or may find useful while performing translation tasks. Like retrospective interviews, process questionnaires can be used for eliciting the general translation strategies respondents or participants use and they can be also task-specific. As for translation process logs, these include guiding questions to which translators respond to record the details of their thinking processes at different stages of the task: before the translation task, during the task and after completing it. Self-report instruments are easy to administer to a large number of respondents, and they are inexpensive and non-threatening (Oxford & Burry-Stock 1995). However, they may be problematic because respondents may be inclined to give the answers they think researchers will like or which will make them seem good translators.

Not many questionnaires have been used in previous translation process research. In most studies, questionnaires were mainly employed for exploring translators' strategy use in a particular task dimension or stage such as revising, post-editing, using sources, or solving problems. For example, the questionnaire Guerberof Arenas (2013) used in her study of post-editing of machine-translated and translation-memory generated texts includes some items concerning translators' revision strategies, for example:

- As I translate, I recheck my translation before going to the next segment.
- Immediately after I finish the translation of one file, I go back and review all my translations.
- After I finish the translation of all files assigned to me, I review the whole batch of files.
- How do you revise fuzzy matches when working in SDL [Software and Documentation Localization] Trados or similar tool?

> *I read the Source, then correct the Target segment.*
> *I read the Target, then the Source segment, then I make the changes.*
> *I look at the changes marked by the tool, then I correct the Target segment.*
> *I read the Target, then I look at changes marked by the tool, then I correct the Target.*
> (Guerberof Arenas 2013, pp. 76–81)

Likewise, Temizöz (2013) used the following items to assess subject-matter experts' versus professional translators' post-editing of machine translated texts:

- Immediately after I finish post-editing the whole text, I go back to all sentences and review them one by one again.
- As I post-edit, I go back and forth and I recheck my post-editing before going to the next sentence.
- Please briefly mention the problems you came across during the post-editing task. (Temizöz 2013, p. 265)

Some other translation process questionnaires have focused on translators' use of sources. Gallego-Hernández (2015), for instance, used a questionnaire

with items assessing Spanish professional translators' use of different translation resources such as monolingual and bilingual dictionaries and corpora,
glossaries, term databases, translation memory corpora, Internet texts, and
machine translation programmes. Additionally, Kim's (2006) study of the use
of extralinguistic knowledge in translation employed a questionnaire with the
following items about translation process problems and problem-solving:

- List the five most difficult problems that you had in the order of difficulty and
  answer the following questions, describing what kind of problems they were
  and how you solved them.
- Problem:
- Do you think you have solved the problem?
- No Yes
- What did you do to solve it? (Kim 2006, p. 300)

It is clear that translation process research still lacks robust and pure
strategy questionnaires. Previously published questionnaires are very few
and include a limited number of questions – mainly quantitative – tapping
translators' strategies. Additionally, they assess translation process aspects
along with translation attitude and ability beliefs. The case is different in
writing process research which has a reasonable number of validated measures
assessing text composing strategies (e.g., Hwang & Lee 2017; Petrić & Czárl
2003; Zhang & Qin 2018; for a review, see Abdel Latif 2021). Therefore, due
attention should be paid to developing strategy questionnaires that assess the
multiple dimensions of the translation process and can be used in different
research settings.

Process logs are not commonly used in translation process research. Daniel
Gile is one of the few researchers who used process logs in translation studies.
Gile (2004) introduced Integrated Problem and Decision Reporting (IPDR)
which is a systematic way for collecting written retrospective data about trans-
lators' problems and their translation problem-solving (Gile 2004). According to
Gile (2004), IPDR is implemented as a translation process data source as follows:

> IPDR's distinctive features arise from the fact that this report on problems
> encountered, on steps taken to solve them, and on the rationale for the final
> decisions made, either in the form of footnotes or as a set of comments and
> explanations which follow the translation, is an integral part of translation
> assignments. While IPDR is only one way to obtain this information, it collects
> it systematically, in written form, from the students, without cues from the
> instructor except the initial instruction and feedback when reports are
> inadequate. . . . [It does] not require any particular reporting format, but besides
> reporting all problems, [research participants] must include full references of

sources consulted, and preferably the context in which target-language terms or expressions which they chose were found (generally a sentence, sometimes a whole paragraph). ... In the reporting phase, the students report in writing their translation problems, action and decisions and hand in their assignments. (Gile 2004, pp. 3–7)

In light of Gile's description, the translation process data obtained from IPDR – or any other similar process logs – can be collected in an individual and group session, and is mainly analysed qualitatively. Process logs help researchers obtain data on written text production processes over a long time (Greene & Higgins 1994) and to observe any potential changes in participants' strategies (Faigley et al. 1985). Additionally, they are regarded as a convenient way for collecting retrospective data which is not very time-consuming to analyse (Hansen 2006). Despite this, not all research participants are able to complete these logs appropriately and regularly in their everyday study or work contexts. Besides, some research participants may have an additional cognitive load if they are to complete the process log and the translation task synchronously.

3.4 Which Data Source(s) to Use?

The issues discussed in subsections 3.1, 3.2, and 3.3 clearly indicate that each data source has its strengths and weaknesses. Therefore, there is no best single source of data about the translation process. Given that each source can reveal different dimensions about translation cognition, it is important to use those appropriate for the research purpose and context. For example, think-aloud protocols may be a more reliable source for modelling translation processes, whereas computer keystroke logging will be a better option for collecting data about temporal aspects (e.g., pause duration and frequency) and revising behaviours. Meanwhile, semi-structured interviews and researcher's observation may fit well within the ethnographic approach which involves researching the long-term changes and challenges in translation processes in workplace environments (see, e.g., Asare (2016); Risku (2014; 2017)).

Triangulation – that is, collecting data using more than one data source – has become a common methodological feature in translation process research. It was Jakobsen (1999) who first introduced triangulation into translation process research. It is generally noted that translation process studies have increasingly implemented data source combination; for instance, by combining think-aloud protocols with interviews, keystroke logging or screen recording, triangulating keystroke logged data with eye-tracking, screen recording or retrospective interviews, and combining interviews with screen recording, questionnaires or researcher's observation. Matsumoto (1994) recommends using one of four data triangulation types by combining: (a) introspective with retrospective data sources; (b) different retrospective data sources; (c) retrospective data sources with product data; or (d) retrospective with observational sources. While some translation process studies used two sources only (e.g., Angelone 2010b; Englund Dimitrova 2005), others relied upon three sources (Faber & Hjort-Pedersen 2009) or more (Göpferich 2009). When deciding upon data triangulation, it is important to select the triangulation approach that helps in collecting the data covering the translation process dimensions addressed by the study.

4 Translation Process Research Developments in Four Decades

Since its beginning in the mid-1980s, translation process research has witnessed changing trends. Alves and Hurtado Albir (2017) refer to four phases in translation process research; each one is marked by some methodological orientations. These phases are as follows:

- The think-aloud protocol research phase (mid 1980s to mid 1990s) in which the focus was on the whole translation process, collecting data from a small number of participants, and using non-systematic research designs;
- The multi-methodological paradigm or data triangulation phase (late 1990s to mid 2000s) which witnessed introducing technological data sources such as keystroke logging and screen recording, and using research designs with greater rigor and more statistical analyses;
- The methodological consolidation paradigm phase (2005–2010) which saw the introduction of eye-tracking in translation process research and the use of more robust designs and inferential statistics; and
- The inter-disciplinary and interactive translation tools phase (early 2010s to the present time) in which translation process research has focused on studying human-computer interaction and making more use of key-logging and eye-tracking technologies.

As noted, these changing methodological orientations concur with the issues discussed in Section 3 about the chronological developments in using data sources in translation process research.

Researchers have studied translators' processes from two angles: the macro angle or investigating the whole translation process, and the micro angle which involves examining a component or specific processing features in it. Most studies researching the translation process either from a macro or micro angel have normally investigated their relationship with some explanatory variables such as:

- Translation competence or expertise: for example student versus professional translators, or novice versus expert translators;
- Translation directionality, that is, translation from one's first language to the second language versus translation from one's second language to the first;
- Characteristics of source text features (e.g., source texts with varied difficulty levels) or translation task types (e.g., translation under time pressure versus translation under no time limit).

Researching the translation process from a macro angel was particularly dominant in early translation process research (e.g., Jääskeläinen 1989; Königs 1987; Krings 1988; Séguinot 1989). This research strand has also continued in many studies published in later decades but these studies focused on other process dimensions. For example, Heeb (2016) examined translators' processes through analysing their attention to the literal transfer of linguistic units (words, phrases, and sentences), and to the text quality aspects such as style and cohesion. PACTE (2019) also analysed translation process data in terms of the time spent on translation tasks, and the translation process competence.

Studies dealing with a particular component or processing element/dimension in the translation have focused on several issues, including: problem-solving, reading behaviours, source use, revision, cognitive attention distribution, translation process styles, and strategy instruction. In the following subsections, selected research on these translation process dimensions is briefly highlighted. Reviewing these research issues could be helpful in understanding the proposed translation process modelling given in the following section.

4.1 Translation Problem-Solving Processes

The translation process by its nature is a problem-solving activity. As implied in Section 2, some researchers view translation strategies as procedures for solving problems (e.g., Krings 1986; Lörscher 1992). Due to the nature of the translation process, the most common problem type translators are expected to encounter is lexical problems. Mondahl and Jensen (1996) note that translators solve the lexical problems they encounter using one of two strategies: (a) retaining the communicative goal of the source text part by finding a lexical alternative close to it (i.e., achievement strategy); and (b) simplifying the meaning of the source text part due to inability to find an acceptable equivalent to it (reduction strategy).

Some published works have focused particularly on conceptualizing or modelling translators' problem-solving processes. Such works, for instance, include the ones reported by Krings (1986), Lörscher (1991), Wilss (1996), and Shih (2015). In all these works, the researchers have tried to depict the potential steps or strategies for solving translation problems (see detailed modelling examples in the next section). Regarding decision-making in translation problem-solving, Shih (2015) states that:

> [T]ranslators normally focus on evaluating one dominant translation solution at a time. In fact, it was found that translators follow the cycle of evaluating solutions one by one until they find a satisfactory solution or, alternatively, they may decide to postpone their quest for a satisfactory solution, at least temporarily. (Shih 2015, p. 84)

With the increasing use of keystroke logging and eye-tracking in translation process studies, researchers have started to investigate the association between translators' pausing and their problem-solving. In most studies, these two technology-aided observation data sources are combined with translators' stimulated retrospective accounts. Translators' long pauses are normally interpreted as signals of their problem-solving processes (Muñoz Martín & Olalla-Soler 2022). For reviews of research on this issue, see Kumpulainen (2015) and Muñoz Martín and Cardona Guerra (2019).

Additionally, other studies have looked at the correlates of translators' problem-solving strategies. Araghian, Ghonsooly, and Ghanizadeh (2018), for instance, combined think-aloud protocols and keystroke logging in exploring the correlation between translators' problem-solving and their self-efficacy levels. Núñez and Bolaños-Medina (2018) also examined how translators' intrinsic motivation and competence predict their self-perceived problem-solving efficacy.

4.2 Translators' Reading Behaviours

While completing translation tasks, translators spend considerable time not only reading target- and source-text parts but also reading related language and information sources. Each reading type or behaviour translators perform has a strategic purpose. As Hvelplund (2017) explains, translation reading is different from normal reading comprehension; it involves reading the source text intensely and thoroughly prior to finding its target text equivalent.

In the two early decades of translation process research, translators' reading was generally studied as a part of the whole translation process. This can be noted, for instance, in Krings (1986) and Lörscher's (1991) works in which reading represents a component or strategy of their proposed translation process frameworks. An early study focusing solely on reading was reported by Shreve et al. (1993) who examined translators' source text reading processing. To address this issue, they used quantitative measures through calculating clause reading time and perceived translation difficulty. They asked 10 translation students to read a text on a computer screen and to translate it. After reading the text, the students were asked to circle the text they perceived would be difficult to translate, and to indicate the cause of the difficulty. Shreve and colleagues found a diversity in their participant translators' reading comprehension processing. These translators were also interested in lower linguistic levels while reading the source text. They conclude that 'the translator's reading of a text may be to some extent more thorough and deliberate than that of an ordinary reader' (p. 36).

The introduction of eye-tracking in translation process research has opened a novel window for studying translators' reading behaviours. Jakobsen and Jensen's (2008) work is perhaps the first published in-depth eye-tracking study of translators' reading. They compared professional and student translators' reading of four similar text types with different purposes: comprehension, preparation for translation, immediate oral translation (i.e., sight translation), and immediate written translation. Their eye-tracking data revealed that while the student translators paid more visual attention to the source text than the target one, the professional translators paid more visual attention to the target text. It was also found that the translators spent more time reading during text translation as compared to other reading tasks.

Other eye-tracking studies have investigated translators' text reading from different angles. For example, Schaeffer et al. (2017) collected eye-tracking data to compare reading for comprehension and reading for translation. They also manipulated the number of target words potentially to be included in the translation of a source word. They found a significant effect for translation task manipulation on total reading time and reading frequency. In another study, Hvelplund (2017) used eye-tracking data in studying the cognitive activities underlying the following four translation reading types: source text reading, source text reading during typing, current target text reading, and emerging target text reading. He found significant differences among the four reading types. Hvelplund concludes that 'the traditional [source text-target text] dichotomy in translation research should be complemented with further itemisation of the types of reading' (Hvelplund 2017, p. 74). In a recent eye-tracking study, Mizowaki, Ogawa and Yamada (2023) explored the reading behaviours involved in two different translation revision conditions: linear translation where the word order of the source text and target text is similar; and non-linear translation where the word order of the source text and target text is dissimilar. Their study showed that in the non-linear translation condition translators expended greater monolingual and bilingual reading efforts.

4.3 Translators' Information Source Use

Resourcing or looking for information in linguistic and non-linguistic sources is part and parcel of translators' tasks. It is generally regarded an instrumental sub-competence in translators' work (Kuznik & Olalla-Soler 2018). Translators' workspace has excitingly changed in the last twenty decades as they now have access not only to traditional printed sources but also to various electronic and online ones (Sycz-Opoń 2019). Such changes in translators' workspace have been accompanied by a considerable amount of research on their use of information sources.

Some studies have addressed translators' source use from a survey angle. For example, Hirci (2012) explored Slovene–English translation difficulties and how they are influenced by the availability versus unavailability of bilingual and monolingual printed and electronic references. Hirci's study drew upon pre- and post-experiment questionnaires to collect data about the student participants' task-specific source use and their evaluation of the translation tools and information sources they use in translation. Kuznik and Olalla-Soler (2018) also conducted a longitudinal study to examine translation students' source use process skills through measuring the total numbers and types of references consulted, and the stage and duration of source use. The students' source use profiles were correlated with their translation process and product aspects. In a later study, Sycz-Opoń (2019) used think-aloud, observation and computer screen data to look at student translators' information-seeking behaviours while converting legal texts from English into Polish. The data of this study was analysed in terms of 'the information most often looked-up in sources, the sources most often consulted, the level of satisfaction with source consultation, the reasons for non-satisfaction, and the problems commonly encountered during the search for information' (Sycz-Opoń 2019, p. 152).

Other studies have focused only on translators' real-time use of digital sources. In such studies, we can note how technological advances have influenced researchers' methodological choice as they have mainly depended on computer-aided observation tools, such as keystroke logging and eye-tracking. For example, Bundgaard and Christensen (2019) combined keystroke logs with interviews in their investigation of translators' source consultations in the post-editing tasks of English–Danish machine-translated technical texts. The digital sources their participants consulted include: concordances, termbases, reference texts, Webpages, and online and offline dictionaries. In three studies,

Hvelplund (2017, 2019, 2023) used eye-tracking and/or screen recording data to look at different issues associated with translators' use of digital sources. The digital sources translators accessed in the studies varied slightly but included: bilingual and monolingual dictionaries, search engines, reference works and websites, and terminology and conversion tools. In the first study, Hvelplund (2017) compared translators' use of digital resources while drafting and revising their texts. In the second study, Hvelplund (2019) explored the patterns of translators' source use and how these patterns relate to the flow of the translation process. This study showed that digital sources are used during several translation stages, in one of the following patterns: source text – digital sources – source text, source text – digital sources – target text, target text – digital resource – source text, and target text – digital sources – target text. In a more recent study, Hvelplund (2023) examined the relationship between European Union (i.e., institutional) translators' source use and their cognitive attention distribution. The translators were found to spend about a quarter of translation task time interacting with digital sources.

4.4 Translators' Revisions

In the last two decades, growing attention has been given to researching the changes made to the translated texts. Prior to the 2000s, researchers examined revision as a sub-component of the translation process. With the emergence of machine-translation and translation memory systems, researchers have explored the cognitive acts involved in changing different types of translated outputs. Jakobsen (2018) tried to draw a distinction among the cognitive acts of these text types as follows:

> The distinction just made between revision, editing, and post-editing is becoming more and more blurred with the use of translation systems that combine [translation memory] and [machine-translation], but may still be useful. . . . '[R]evision' [is] . . . used generically to refer to any changes made in a translation, but mainly to refer specifically to changes made in a translation written by a translator, either by the translator (self-revision) or by another person (other-revision). 'Editing' [is] used to refer to changes made by a translator to match suggestions from a [translation memory], and 'post-editing' [is used to] refer to changes made by a translator to suggestions generated by [a machine translation] system, although with the integration of [machine-translation] and [translation memory], this distinction is often lost. (Jakobsen 2018, p. 66)

Research focusing solely on human translation revisions seems to have been published only during the 2000s. The studies reported by Breedveld (2002) and Shih (2006) are perhaps two of the earliest focusing on translators' revision. Two main types of translation revisions can be distinguished: (a) online revisions made during the drafting phase; and (b) end revisions made during the final phase of the translation task (Carl, Dragsted, & Jakobsen 2011; Jakobsen 2018). Like all the areas of translation research, methodological developments can be noted in revision studies. For example, the two early translation revision studies Breedveld (2002) and Shih (2006) reported depended on think-aloud protocols and retrospective interviews, respectively, whereas later studies (e.g., Alves & Vale 2011; Schaeffer et al. 2019) used keystroke logging and eye-tracking. Data analysis of translators' revisions also varied depending on the methodology used. For example, Shih (2006) focused on identifying what revision means to translators, the numbers of revisions made, and the aspects checked in revision. On the other hand, Englund Dimitrova (2005) analysed the syntactic, lexical, morphological, content and orthographic revisions made by translators.

It is worth mentioning that most previous translation revision studies have been concerned with translators' self-revision rather than other-revision; the latter type aims mainly at optimizing translated text accuracy and fluency and making sure it conforms to the norms of the target language (Jakobsen 2018); that is, it means revising the text translated by another translator (Jakobsen 2018; Robert & Brunette 2016). Very little attention has been paid to examining the cognitive processes associated with other-revision. Among the few relevant studies published are those reported by Robert (2013, 2014) and Robert and van Waes (2014). A main issue investigated in these studies is comparing bilingual and monolingual other-revision processes and products.

As translation revision has become a more technology-mediated process, an increasing number of studies have focused on examining translators' cognitive processes while editing technology-assisted translated texts. This increase has mainly been associated with the improvements in the quality of machine-translated outputs. The significance of (post-)editing research is that it may reveal the translator's cognitive capacity and the potential human efforts needed when interacting with machine-translated products, and the relationship of such efforts with machine translation errors and source-text features (Jakobsen 2018; Nunes Vieira 2017). Some post-editing translation process studies have adopted a comparative approach by examining the cognitive behaviours used in editing machine-translated texts versus human-translated ones (e.g., Daems et al. 2017; Jia, Carl, & Wang 2019), or investigating professional versus non-professional translators' machine-translated output post-editing strategies (e.g., de Lima Fonseca 2019) or the post-editing processes of outputs translated by different machine translation systems (e.g., Koglin & Cunha 2019); for a review of the issues addressed in post-editing research, see Sun (2019). Compared to its machine-translated post-editing counterpart, relatively less research has dealt with translators' cognitive acts when editing the outputs produced with the aid of translation memory systems. These studies include those reported by Dragsted (2004, 2006), O'Brien (2007), O'Brien, O'Hagan, and Flanagan (2010), and Christensen and Schjoldager (2011). These studies have mostly depended on technology-based observation tools in collecting data.

4.5 Translators' Cognitive Effort Allocation

A considerable number of studies have addressed the cognitive efforts translators allocate to translation processes; this effort allocation is sometimes labelled cognitive attention distribution. According to Gile and Lei (2020), the main reason for studying translators' cognitive effort allocation is to understand 'the link between the effort invested by the translator and his/her performance. . . . The correlation is assumed to be strong for low effort investment; the translation done carelessly will most probably exhibit weaknesses' (Gile & Lei 2020, p. 265).

Methodologically, previous research has investigated translators' effort allocation from different angles such as examining their problem-solving and information processing, the time allocated to different translation phases/processes, and pausing and gaze fixation time. Jääskeläinen (1999), for instance, depended on think-aloud protocols in identifying the verbalization instances signalling professional versus non-professional translators' attention to the following translation process categories: (a) procedural comments and global translation strategies; (b) source text or comprehension; (c) target text processing; and (d) other issues. Jääskeläinen found that her participant translators paid the largest amount of attention to target text processing. Using computer keystroke logging, Jakobsen (2002) probed the time translators allocate to the following three phases: (a) the orientation phase during which the translator reads the whole source text or part of it; (b) the drafting phase in which the translator produces a partial or complete translation draft; and (c) the end revision phase during which the translator revises the translated text draft and tackles newly discovered problems in it. The keystroke logging data in Jakobsen's study showed that the orientation phase made up 3% of the translators' processing time, whereas the drafting and revision phase accounted for 77% and 20%, respectively.

The introduction of eye-tracking in translation process research has offered researchers a different option for studying translators' effort allocation. In their dependence on eye-tracking, translation process researchers have followed the implications drawn from Just and Carpenter's (1980) seminal work which implies the potential of using eye fixations for identifying instances of effortful cognitive processing. For example, the studies reported by Jakobsen and Jensen (2008), Sharmin et al. (2008), and Pavlović and Jensen (2009) compared the differences in eye fixation during source text versus target text reading. These studies found that the latter type of text processing is more cognitively effortful than the former. In a more in-depth study, Hvelplund (2011) combined eye-tracking with keystroke logging data to investigate student and professional translators' cognitive effort allocation to source text processing, target text processing, and parallel source and target text processing. In his data analysis, Hvelplund focused on (a) attention or time measurement units with identifiable boundaries of cognitive processing (or implied problem-solving), and these were marked by eye movement data (fixations and saccades) and typing activities; and (b) attention or effort allocation shifts indicated by shifts in visual attention. Hvelplund's study revealed that the translators paid significantly more attention to target text reformulation than to source text comprehension, and that the professional translators undertook more automatic processing than the student translators whose heavier cognitive load was indicated by their attention switching between cognitive processes.

An important issue related to studying translators' cognitive effort allocation is whether translation is a parallel process or not. Parallel processing in translation occurs when its processes overlap, for example when translators perform two processing tasks synchronously with one task at the centre of attention and another undertaken subconsciously; conversely, sequential processing occurs if there is no overlap (Balling, Hvelplund, & Sjørup 2014). In general, parallel processing in translation is viewed as a dimension in skilled translators' performance as it indicates its automaticity (Hvelplund 2011). Some eye-tracking studies (e.g., Balling, Hvelplund, & Sjørup 2014; Yang, Wang, & Fan 2022) provide evidence for parallel processing in translation.

Despite the increase in published research on translator effort allocation, some concerns have been raised about the methodological approaches used in it. For example, Hvelplund (2011) suggests that since think-aloud protocols data can only reflect a limited portion of translators' processing, they may not show the focus of their attention reliably. On the other hand, Gile and Lei (2020) consider that while eye-tracking data indicators such as gaze duration and pausing may inform us about translators' cognitive effort intensity, they cannot accurately indicate the specific sub-processes within each translation component or the causes of translators' behaviours. It is believed, therefore, that triangulation can help in data validation and enrichment in studies of translators' effort allocation.

4.6 Translation Process Styles

A translation process area yet to be given due attention is translators' cognitive styles. According to Mossop (2000), translation process style is the translator' general translation production procedures or habits, the order in which translators perform cognitive processes while translating, and how they distribute them over the phases of the translation task. It can also be defined as the particular recurrent tendencies and individual behavioural characteristics or profiles noted in the translator's processing (Carl, Dragsted, & Jakobsen 2011; Dragsted & Carl 2013). What is meant by translators' cognitive styles is explained from Borg's (2018) description of translators' varied approaches to starting the translation task:

> The length and activities performed during [the pre-drafting] phase differ considerably among translators and this variation seems unrelated to translation experience. . . . Some translators jot down words/phrases or carry out research, some read the whole [source text], others browse it quickly, whereas certain translators start translating immediately, skipping this phase altogether. (Borg 2018, p. 80)

The importance of studying translators' styles is that it provides information about the most effective ways of completing translation tasks (Mossop 2000).

Very few studies have focused on translators' cognitive styles. Mossop (2000) is perhaps the first researcher to call for investigating translators' styles. He refers to the possibility of categorizing translators' styles drawing upon Chandler's (1993) taxonomy of writing process styles. He also provides two imaginative illustrative examples of two translators' search for information during the three phases of the translation task (i.e., pre-drafting, drafting, and post-drafting).

The first published empirical attempts to study translators' processing styles are likely the ones reported by Carl, Dragsted, and Jakobsen (2011) and Dragsted and Carl (2013). Their research on translators' styles was influenced by the earlier writing process work by Flower and Hayes (1980), Boehm (1993), Chandler (1993), and van Waes and Schellens (2003). These two studies made use of eye-tracking and keystroke logging data. In the first study, Carl, Dragsted, and Jakobsen (2011) classified translators in terms of their revision as: (a) online revisers: translators making revisions while drafting the target text; (b) end-revisers: translators spending more than 20 per cent of the translation time on revising their first draft; and (b) constant revisers: translators combining both behavioural patterns of revisions. In the second study, Dragsted and Carl (2013) identified other categories of translation styles during the pre-drafting and drafting phases, along with the revision styles mentioned above. In Dragsted and Carl's taxonomy, translators' cognitive styles during the pre-drafting phase include: (a) head-starters: translators who transcribe the target text immediately without any planning; (b) quick planners: translators who read a few words or sentences before transcribing the first target text part; and (c) scanners: the translators who scan the text rapidly. Online planning styles during the drafting phase include: (a) broad-context planners; translators orienting themselves in a broad context, and attending to a sentence or a group of sentences further down in the text part being read or translated; (b) narrow-context planners: translators focusing on a small text part, for example a few words ahead of the text part being translated; and (c) sentence planners: translators preferring to plan one sentence after reading it.

Meanwhile, Alves and Vale (2011) classify their participant translators' cognitive styles drawing on keystroke logging data. Their taxonomy of translators' revision styles include the following categories: (a) drafters: translators who revise the target text in the drafting phase more than in the revision phase; (b) revisers: translators who revise the target text in the revision phase more than in the drafting phase; (c) recursive drafters/revisers: translators who revise the same parts of the source text during the drafting and the revision phases; and (d) non-recursive drafters/revisers: translators who do not revise the same parts of the source text during the drafting and the revision phases.

The exemplary research reviewed in this subsection shows the interesting insights that can be gained from studies on translators' cognitive styles. However, these studies are generally scarce. Ascribing such paucity to the time-consuming nature of and the difficulties involved in this specific translation process research area, Mossop (2000) suggests researchers should start with small-scale studies addressing it. Given that this area is still in its infancy, future relevant studies may investigate the explanatory variables of translators' styles such as task type, and translator's experience.

4.7 Translation Process Training

Though translation process research is based on the assumption that it can enrich translator training by enhancing our understanding of trainees' cognitive behaviours and familiarizing them with effective strategies, not much attention has been given to researching translation process training. Arguably, this low level of attention is associated with a lack of emphasis on integrating process or strategy instruction into translator training. As Pym (2011) notes, 'process-based research ... picks up several aspects that are rarely fore-grounded in the pedagogical models based on products. These include speed, the capacity to distribute effort in terms of risk, the use of external resources ... and ...

reviewing' (Pym 2011, p. 321). This negligence of process training research stands is in sharp contrast to its importance, which lies in raising translator trainees' awareness of their task performance weaknesses and strengths and of effective translation strategies, and helping translation teachers understand trainees' problems (Gile 2009; Massey & Ehrensberger-Dow 2013; Pym 2009).

Some process training literature is mainly prescriptive, that is, confined to providing suggestions for training translators in translation processes. For example, Gile (2009) used his sequential model of the translation process to show how to raise trainee translators' awareness of the effective implementation of source text comprehension and target text reformulation processes. Specifically, he refers to drawing trainees' attention to checking the outcome of their source text comprehension and target text reformulation processes against their linguistic and background knowledge and available resources.

The few available translation process training studies have used different approaches. For example, Alves (2005) reported a pilot study in which the translation processes of 18 student translators were recorded using Translog. The students' retrospective accounts were collected immediately after the translation task during the replay of Translog data. In the following phases, the students listened to their comments, and cross-analysed and discussed them while watching their Translog pausing and segmentation patterns, compared their retrospective comments to the translated texts, and noted the differences between their performance in the drafting and revision phases. The positive outcomes Alves found in this study led him to conclude that process training is a way to bridge the gap between declarative and procedural aspects in translator training. Pym (2009), who drew upon Mossop's (2000) taxonomy of translator styles, also reported using translation task screen-recorded data as a tool for translator training. After collecting this data, Pym asked his participant students to observe and evaluate their translation processes in the following way:

> Play back your screen recording. Try to keep a track of how many seconds you spent on the following tasks: a) technical problems, b) reading, comprehending, c) documentation (web searches), d) translating, drafting, e) reviewing after the drafting (not including the correction of typos as you type). . . . Upload your translations and the analysis of your time-on-tasks, plus brief answers to the following questions: a) What kind of translator are you? (Do you plan first, then do the task, or do you do the task, then make changes?), b) Did any aspect of your translating surprise you? (p.143)

Unlike the previous research, Massey and Ehrensberger-Dow (2011) conducted a translation process training study in which they used more than one observational data source and also collected their data from both students and teachers. Specifically, they gathered a corpus of keystroke logging, eye-tracking, and screen movement data from eight students at four different phases (during their translation degree programme, after completing it, and after gaining professional experience). The eight students were invited back in individual sessions in which they watched anonymously selected recorded sessions of their peers' translation processes, and were asked to provide commentaries on them. Immediately afterwards, the students were interviewed about their own translation processes, and were asked to compare them to those of their peers. Meanwhile, the translation teachers of these students also attended individual interview sessions in which they watched some recorded data of the translation processes and commented on students' translation strategies. The results of Massey and Ehrensberger-Dow's study imply that engaging students and teachers in exploring translation processes in this way resulted in heightening students' awareness of key aspects of the translation process at different levels, fostering students' peer-to-peer learning through allowing them to gain comparative insights into translation strategies, and helping teachers understand students' translation behaviours and realize the potential of using observational data about the translation process as a diagnostic tool in investigating trainees' translation performance.

It may be concluded that translation process training is still in its infancy. On the one hand, the research reported in this regard is scarce. On the other hand, it can best be described as 'pilot' studies, as some of studies were described by the researchers reporting them (e.g., Massey & Ehrensberger-Dow 2011; Pym 2009). It is likely that progress in this research area requires identifying the teachable and non-teachable translation process components, and the processing features translators can use consciously or subconsciously.

5 Modelling the Translation Process

Precise modelling of the translation process might enrich our understanding of it, and enable us to use more reliable frameworks for analysing translation data and developing valid measures for assessing translation cognition and difficulties. A cognitive model of the written text production process is a blueprint or an outline proposing a definition of its architecture and functioning (Alamargot & Chanquoy 2001). In modelling the translation process, researchers try to describe the cognitive acts involved in translating a text and/or explain the factors influencing it. Thus, translation process models differ from translation competence models (e.g., Neubert 1997; PACTE 2000, 2003) which try to identify what constitutes translation expert knowledge and skills and how they are acquired.

The translation process models proposed so far can generally be classified into two categories: (a) global models describing the whole translation process and its main components, and how they interact with each other; and (b) problem-solving models depicting the steps or strategies translators use in solving translation problems. In the writing process area the models proposed by Hayes and colleagues (e.g., Chenoweth & Hayes 2001; Flower & Hayes 1981) and Kellogg (1996) have often been cited and used as frameworks for analysing writers' composing data, whereas in translation studies there are no agreed-upon translation process models researchers commonly use. In the following two subsections, some notable models of the two types are briefly highlighted along with the works covering pertinent issues.

5.1 Components of the Translation Process

As indicated in the above paragraph, global models give descriptions of the whole translation process and the main components it encompasses. Two different approaches can be identified in researchers' conceptualizations of translation process components. First, some researchers have identified the components of the translation process in terms of its phases. An example of this classification type is Jakobsen's (2002) above-mentioned taxonomy (see Section 4.5) in which the translation process is divided into the orientation, drafting, and end-revision phases. Mossop (2000) also used an earlier similar translation process taxonomy with the following three phases: (a) pre-drafting phase: exploring the source text and getting acquainted with it; (b) drafting: composing the target text; and (c) post-drafting: reviewing and making any necessary changes in the target text. While these phase-based taxonomies have their rationale, they do not consider the recursive nature of the translation process. In other words, they suggest that translators implement these phases in a linear way, an indication contradicting the well-acknowledged assumption about the recursiveness of the translation process.

The second but much more common way to classify the translation process components is to categorize them in terms of their processing nature. According to Hurtado Albir and Alves (2009), translation is conceptualized in light of the interpretive theory as a process of three components: understanding or interpreting the source text, deverbalization or target text synthesis, and re-expression or linguistic formulation. Translation process researchers have further elaborated on these three components. For example, Gerloff (1986) identifies the following translation process components: problem identification, linguistic analysis, information retrieval, information search and selection, text reasoning and contextualisation, and task monitoring. Krings (1986) also suggests that the translation process encompasses four components: comprehending the source text message and using sources, retrieving equivalent text parts, monitoring the equivalent generated, and decision-making and reduction. For Shreve and Koby (1997), there are four main components in the translation process; these are: comprehending and interpreting the source text message, reformulating the source text message into the target language, and expressing the transposed message in the target language. On the other hand, Hvelplund (2011) believes that the translation process can generally be conceptualized as encompassing two main types of processing: source text processing and target text processing. Source text processing involves reading and comprehending a word/sentence part through fixating it, identifying physical properties of its letters, and lexically analysing it. As for target text processing, it entails reformulating and transcribing.

Some models have also provided global conceptualizations of the translation process components. For example, in Bell's (1991) model, the translation process is composed of two phases: source text analysis and target text synthesis. The two phases depend on short-term and long-term memories. As noted in Figure 2, source text analysis starts with the visual recognition of a word/ sentence part which is then analysed syntactically, semantically, and pragmatically. Through these analyses, which are combined with lexical searches, the translator tries to generate a semantic representation of the source text part drawing upon some kind of planning. Once the semantic representation is approved by the monitor, the translator starts synthesizing the target text part pragmatically, semantically, and syntactically; all the three text synthesis types are also mediated by lexical searches and end with transcribing the target text part. Bell points out that processing the source or target text at syntactic, semantic, and pragmatic levels has no fixed order as the translator's regular online revision is associated with processing regression.

On the other hand, Danks and Griffin's (1997) model suggests that the translation process encompasses source text comprehension, target text reformulation, evaluation, and target text production. Their model provides a detailed account of source text reading in particular. According to this model, for the mental representation of the source text message to be formed, the translator draws upon background knowledge in processing its orthographic and lexical features, and analysing its phrasal, propositional, and sentential context. The model also proposes that the translator evaluates the reformulated text in terms of its meaning, and how it meets their intent, the source text writer's message, and user's expectation.

Gile (2009) also proposed a sequential model in which he views translation as a process with two-phase processing operations as set out in Figure 3. According to this model, each translation unit – which could be a single word, a sentence

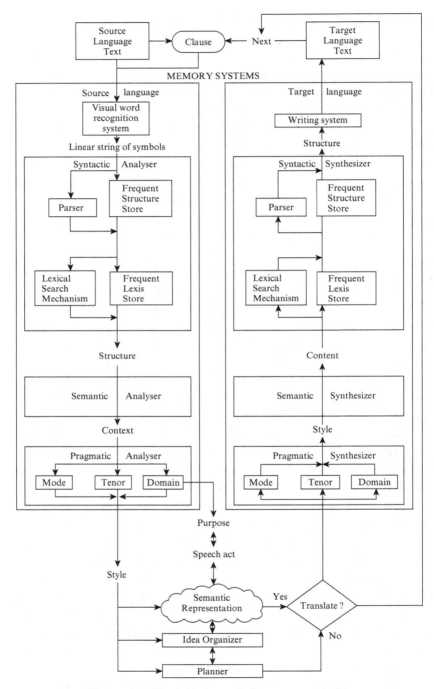

Figure 2 Bell's (1991) translation process model.

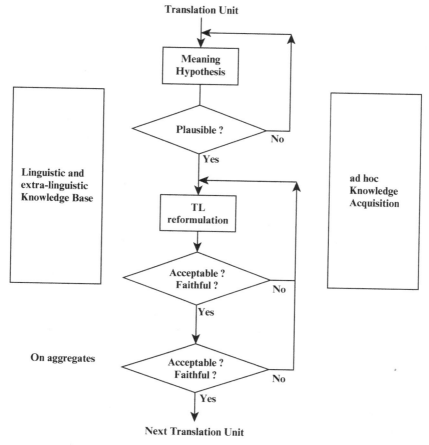

Figure 3 Gile's (2009) sequential model of the translation process.

part, a sentence, or more – is processed through two phases: comprehending the source text and reformulating the target text. After reading the source text part, the translator temporarily assigns a meaning to it; this meaning is either approved or rejected by the monitor. Once accepted, the translator starts formulating the target text, and the reformulated text is also to be approved by the monitor. The two phases of comprehension and reformulation are mediated and optimized by decision-making which normally depends on knowledge available to the translator from two sources: (a) their knowledge base comprising linguistic knowledge of the source and target texts and background extra-linguistic knowledge; and (b) their task-specific or ad hoc knowledge.

More recently, Oster (2017) provided a translation process model adapted from Levelt's (1999) theory of lexical access in speech production. Oster's translation process model includes the following components: source text reading, comprehension and conceptualization, and target text formulation, monitoring, and articulating the message. Oster explains the roles of these processes as follows:

> Translators read the text, then link the orthographical and phonological information to lexical and grammatical information, and access meaning. Next, translators might change the message before they choose lexical and grammatical information in the target language in order to verbalize the message. They finally articulate the message or write it down. . . . [M]onitoring of the production of words takes place after the first activation of words in the mental lexicon, [and] it already has an impact on the production before the first articulation occurs. (Oster 2017, pp. 25–30)

Despite the important insights gained from the global models reviewed in this subsection, they have not explicated some roles of particular translation sub-processes or components. For example, the roles of monitoring and information search are only partially explained. More importantly, the models do not show clearly how translation processes/strategies are organized and coordinated. Meanwhile, the processes of target text reviewing and revision are rarely included. Overall, the translation process involves more components and more strategic details than those described in the above-mentioned global models. More details are given in the following two subsections.

5.2 Modelling Translation Problem-Solving Processes

Since translation by nature is a problem-solving activity, many attempts have been made to depict the processes involved in solving translation problems. The importance of these models is that they reveal more detailed information about the complexities of the translation process. Krings (1986) developed an early translation problem-solving model, shown in Figure 4. In Krings's model, the translation process is viewed as a problem-solving operation triggered by encountering a problem with no satisfactory solution. In order to solve the translation problem, the translator makes use of the following types of strategies:

- Problem identification or analysis strategies: reflecting upon the problem and analysing it using reasoning, inferencing, and available references.
- Retrieval strategies: drawing upon inter-lingual association, the semantic analysis of the source-language text item, and references to produce the target translation equivalent.
- Monitoring strategies: evaluating the translation equivalent(s) generated and deciding whether to accept them or not; if the translator does not accept the proposed solution, they may look for a reduction in the target text (such as dispensing with a particular semantic feature).

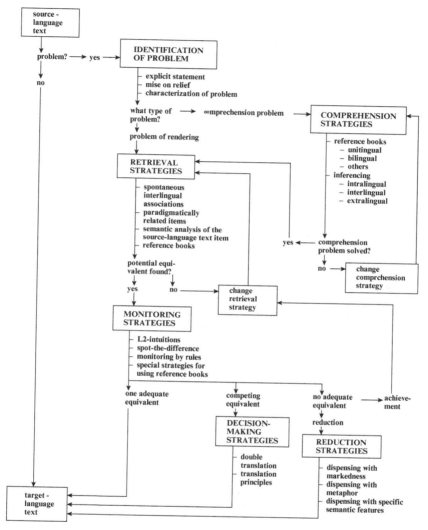

Figure 4 Krings's (1986) translation problem-solving model.

Another early conceptualization of translation problem-solving was proposed by Lörscher (1992) who argues that translation strategies have their starting-point when the translator realizes a problem, and ending-point when the translator finds a solution or realizes that the proposed solution is inappropriate. Between realizing the translation problem and finding its solution or discovering its insolubility, further cognitive operations may occur. According to Lörscher (1992), the translator may produce multiple translation versions due to solving the translation problem unsuccessfully at the first attempt, trying to

optimize the target language text through finding a better alternative version. Lörscher differentiates between two categories of translation strategy elements: the original elements which are part of strategic or problem-solving phases of the translation process and the potential elements which are part of non-strategic phases of the process. Drawing upon think-aloud data, Lörscher found the following 22 translation strategies in the two categories:
Original elements of translation strategies

RP : Realizing a translation problem

VP : Verbalizing a translation problem

SP : Search for a (possibly preliminary) solution to a translation problem

SP : Solution to a translation problem

PSP : Preliminary solution to a translation problem

SPa,b,c : Parts of a solution to a translation problem

SP0 : A solution to a translation problem is still to be found (0)

SP=0 : Negative (0) solution to a translation problem

PSL : Problem in the reception of the SL text

Potential elements of translation strategies

MSL : Monitoring (verbatim repetition) of SL text segments

MTL : Monitoring (verbatim repetition) of TL text segments

REPHR.SL : Rephrasing (paraphrasing) of SL text segments

REPHR.TL : Rephrasing (paraphrasing) of TL text segments

CHECK : Discernible testing (=Checking) of a preliminary solution to a translation problem

OSL : Mental organization of SL text segments

OTL : Mental organization of TL text segments

REC : Reception (first reading) of SL text segments

[TS]com : Comment on a Text Segment

TRANS : Transposition of lexemes or combinations of lexemes

T : Translation of Text Segments without any problems involved

→ T2,3,... n : Conceiving a second, third, etc., translation version

ORG : Organization of translational discourse

(Lörscher 1992, p. 429; Lörscher 2002, pp. 100–101; Lörscher 2005, p. 607)

In Kiraly's (1995) model of translation problem-solving, translation is viewed as a process relying upon three elements: (a) information sources stored in the long-term memory such as translation-related and non-translation-related schemata, and lexico-semantic and syntactic knowledge; (b) the relatively uncontrolled processing centre in which translation operations are performed intuitively and less consciously; and (c) the relatively controlled processing centre in which these operations are performed strategically and more consciously. Kiraly states that the translator's mind is the information-processing system in which the translation product is formed as a result of the interaction between uncontrolled and controlled operations depending on the information sources stored in the long-term memory. He also explains that a translation problem occurs in the uncontrolled processing centre when the translator is unable to find a tentative translation output; in this case, the problem is attended to in the controlled processing centre. In case the translation problem remains unsolved, it goes back to the intuitive processing centre where long-term memory information interacts with source text input subconsciously.

In conceptualizing the problem-solving process in translation, Wilss (1996) draws a distinction between two knowledge types: declarative knowledge or knowing what, and procedural knowledge or knowing how. According to Wilss (1994), decision-making in the translation process is an information-processing feature through which the translator's cognitive system interacts with their linguistic and non-linguistic knowledge bases, translation task specifications, and text-specific problem space. The interaction among these factors enables the translator to form an internal representation of the translation problem and a solution for it. For Wilss (1996), decision-making in the translation process involves the following six steps: identifying a problem, clarifying it, searching for and retrieving relevant information, choosing a problem-solving strategy, selecting a solution, and evaluating the solution. Wilss explains that with each of these six steps some further problem(s) may occur, thus causing a delay or an interruption in solving the translation problem.

Robert (2014) developed a conceptualization of problem representation in translation revision. She differentiates between ill-defined and well-defined problem representations. The former representation type occurs if the translator has a vague detection of the problem, or a rejection of the translation.

The latter occurs in the form of an intentional, maxim-based or rule-based diagnosis of the problem.

Finally, Shih (2015) proposed a translation end-revision problem-solving process model which is adapted from Wilss's (1996) model. This adapted model fills a modelling gap related to translation problem-solving and decision-making during end-revisions. As Figure 5 shows, the steps of the translation end-revision problem-solving process in Shih's (2015) model are: identifying a problem, defining it, generating a solution, testing or evaluating the solution, accepting the solution or rejecting it, and confirming the decision made through bolstering or de-emphasizing.

The models reviewed in this subsection highlight the central role of monitoring in the translator's decision-making when solving translation problems (Kiraly 1995; Krings 1986; Lörscher 1992; Shih 2015; Wilss 1996). This role

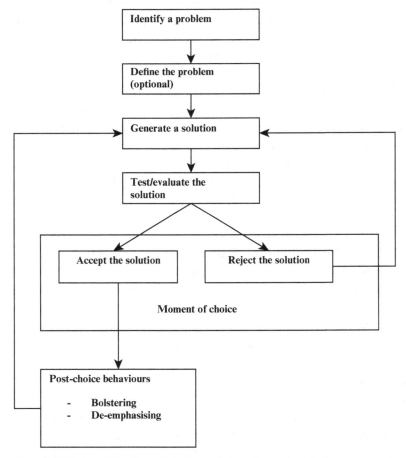

Figure 5 Shih's (2015) model of the end-revision decision-making and problem-solving process.

is also indicated in some global conceptualizations of the translation problem (e.g., Bell 1991; Gerloff 1986; Gile 2009; Oster 2017). Other works have discussed in detail how translators monitor their cognitive processes (e.g., Carl & Dragsted 2012; Hansen 2003; Oster 2017; Schaeffer & Carl 2013; Tirkkonen-Condit 2005). Collectively, these works associate monitoring use with translators' evaluation of proposed or transcribed target text alternatives and taking decisions upon them. Tirkkonen-Condit (2005), for instance, states that 'the monitor's function is to trigger off conscious decision-making to solve the problem' (Tirkkonen-Condit 2005, p. 408). Bell (1991), Gile (2009), and Oster (2017) also view that translators use monitoring for evaluating the proposed target text alternatives (or target text representation) before transcribing them. Arguably, these conceptualizations of monitoring use in the translation process are limited. The next subsection highlights this issue.

5.3 Towards a Remodelling of the Translation Process

While the global and problem-solving models reviewed in subsections 5.1 and 5.2 have significantly widened our understanding of the translation process, some gaps remain unaddressed in translation process modelling. Particular translation processing features have neither been included nor fully explained in these models. For translation process modelling to be complete, we need to explicate the roles of the monitoring, information search, target text reviewing and revision components in translators' processes.

Monitoring plays a far greater role in the translation process than indicated in previous models and relevant literature. Its role is not only limited to evaluating translation alternatives and problems and taking decisions upon them. In writing process theories, monitoring is generally viewed as the strategist and coordinating component which allows the writer to move from one composing process to another (Flower & Hayes 1981). It is also defined as checking on the information being processed and how it is being processed (Ruiz-Funes 1999). Moreover, writing process literature indicates that monitoring is the component responsible for organizing text composing processes and managing them, evaluating the proposed or written idea/text, and also regulating one's motivation during writing (see Abdel Latif 2021). Likewise, it is assumed that translators not only monitor their source text understanding, and proposed or transcribed target text production, but they also monitor their task performance procedures, and how they are implemented. Accordingly, there is a need for expanding the definition of monitoring in translation process research.

Similarly, the role of resourcing or the search for information is not fully described in previous translation process models. Some but not all of the conceptualizations reviewed above include an information search element (e.g., Bell 1991; Gerloff 1986; Krings 1986; Oster 2017; Wilss 1996). These conceptualizations generally tackle translators' linguistic (mostly lexical) information retrieval, but do not refer to their use of sources. Thus, these conceptualizations are inconsistent with the research findings indicating the large amount of time translators spend on using information sources (see Section 4.3). During translation tasks, translators look for lexical or grammatical items, and they may also have to find information about the meaning of some unfamiliar source text words/ phrases prior to finding target text equivalents. In searching for these different information types, translators depend first on retrieval of the information stored in their long-term memory, and – if their memory retrieval attempts fail – they use external information sources. We can conclude, therefore, that translators' search for information either in the form of memory retrieval or source use constitutes a central part which takes much of translation task time (e.g., Hvelplund 2017, 2019, 2023). As a result, we need to demystify translators' information search, and characterize it as a separate component in translation process modelling.

Additionally, we cannot ignore reviewing and revision when modelling translators' processing. While performing their tasks, translators review the proposed target text (i.e., check how it matches the intended meaning in the source text prior to transcribing it), and also the transcribed text (through verifying its meaning, and scanning and reading it). In their think-aloud protocol data, Mondahl and Jensen (1996) noted translators' use of the former review type (i.e., verifying the meaning of the proposed target text) through back translation. Specifically, they found that translators try to identify 'differences between the source text and a potential translation equivalent. ... [And they] may also test adequacy by "translating back" to the source text in order to check whether the two expressions are similar' (Mondahl & Jensen 1996, p. 103). While this view of the role of reviewing in the translation process concurs with some writing models (e.g., Abdel Latif 2021; Chenoweth & Hayes 2001), translation modelling literature generally implies that reviewing is an embedded process in translators' text production (Danks & Griffin 1997; Gile 2009; Oster 2017) or revision (e.g., Shih 2015; Wilss 1996). The gradual disappearance of the think-aloud method in translation process studies (see Sun (2011)) and researchers' over-dependence on keystroke logging and eye-tracking have not helped in distinguishing translations reviewing from text production or revision; arguably, the distinction between these processes can be made through gathering concurrent verbalizations rather than keystroke logging and/or eye-movement data only. For a better modelling of the translation process, we need to conceptualize or characterize the three processes (monitoring, target text reviewing, and revision) as separate components due to the following reasons: (a) monitoring is responsible for supervising all translation processes and procedures by initiating, and approving or rejecting them; therefore, it interferes in all translation processes rather than in reviewing and revision only; (b) reviewing the target text through reading or scanning may not necessarily result in changing it; (c) translators may change the target text without reading or scanning it (for example, in case of realizing an error made while transcribing); and d) revision entails many complexities as translators make changes in the target text at the syntactic, lexical, morphological, content and orthographic levels through additions, omission or substitution (see Englund Dimitrova 2005).

Overall, the issues reviewed and discussed in this section indicate a need for a different translation process model which provides a more detailed and clear-cut description of its components and shows how they are managed and coordinated. In this work, a translation process model is proposed to meet these requirements. The proposed model is adapted from Abdel Latif's (2021) writing process model given in Figure 6. This adaptation is based on the assumption that writing and translation processes are similar and share a number of common phases and characteristics (Dam-Jensen & Heine 2013; Göpferich & Nelezen 2014; Immonen 2006; Kobayashi & Rinnert 1992; Risku, Milosevic & Pein-Weber 2016; Robert & Brunette 2016; Uzawa 1996). Risku, Milosevic, and Pein-Weber (2016), for instance, point out that:

> The tasks of writing and translation show several similarities in the challenges they pose and the processes they include. ... As far as the phases are concerned, ... both writing and translation projects contain planning, drafting and revision phases. In addition, [there are] phases of organization and research in both activities. ... [T]he micro-processes of text production are indeed similar in writing and translation, whereas organizational processes, content planning and the social network play a more dominant role in writing than in translation. (pp. 47–48/63)

Likewise, Immonen (2006) found that both writing and translation require approximately the same time proportion in the task orientation phase, though translation needs more revision and monitoring behaviours. Noting such common characteristics in writing and translation cognition, Dam-Jensen and Heine (2013) suggest that these forms of cognitive research could benefit from each other (p. 90). With regard to process modelling in the two fields, they specifically state that:

> Writing research and translation research have developed different models of phases and strategies. A fundamental line of new research could be to theoretically compare and discuss these models. [Since] models for adaptation have not been developed, so an emergent line of research would be to discuss the

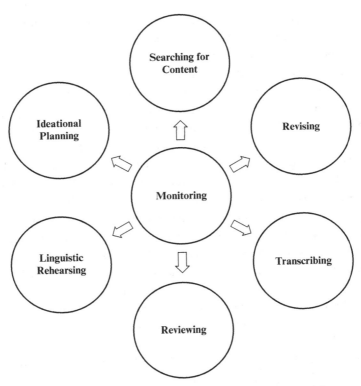

Figure 6 Abdel Latif's (2021) writing process model.

extent to which the models of writing and translation apply to adaptation, and the extent to which the concept of adaptation might constitute a suitable bridge between the fields. (pp. 95–96)

As noted in Figure 6, Abdel Latif's (2021) writing process model describes text composing as a process comprising seven sub-processes or components. In this model, monitoring is the central process responsible for managing and organizing the process of text composition, and evaluating the proposed or written idea/text and writing procedures. With these multiple functions, monitoring plays the role of working memory in the writing process. It encompasses the following types of writing process strategies: (a) task-management: setting goals for writing procedures and observing task time and reminders; (b) ideational and metalinguistic reasoning; (c) evaluation: identifying a problem, approving or rejecting proposed writing alternatives and procedures; and (d) motivation or emotion regulation. This expanded definition suggests that the following six writing process components are monitored:

- *Searching for content*: activating memory retrieval and using external sources for finding what to write (searching for ideas) or for how to write it (searching for the target linguistic alternative(s)).
- *Ideational planning*: proposing ideas for writing at the essay or whole text, paragraph or sentence level.
- *Linguistic rehearsing*: proposing the linguistic form of the sentence or sentence part to be written prior to deciding whether or not to include it in the text.
- *Reviewing*: verifying the meaning of the proposed or written text and scanning and reviewing the text written.
- *Transcribing*: translating the proposed text into written language for the first time using a pen/pencil and paper, or typing tools.
- *Text revising*: changing the written text; writers' revisions can be classified in terms of their operation type (addition, deletion, and substitution), their timing (online and post-writing), and the linguistic unit level changed (revising a sentence, a phrase or a word; editing grammar, spelling, or punctuation).

For detailed definitions of these writing process components and their think-aloud protocol examples, see Abdel Latif (2021).

Based on Abdel Latif's (2021) writing process model and the insights gained from the translation process literature reviewed in this work, the model proposed in this work provides a more detailed description of the translation process, and shows how its components interact with each other. As Figure 7 illustrates, the model depicts translation as a process with the following seven components or sub-processes: monitoring, source text representation, searching for information, target text rehearsing, target text reviewing, transcribing, and revising. Monitoring in this proposed model assumes the role of working memory as it is the organizer and coordinator of the whole translation process and its other components. It initiates the goals of the translation task and its subtasks or parts, allows the translator to move from one sub-process or step to another, forces the translator to accept or reject the proposed or transcribed target text, identifies any potential problem(s) in it, and alerts them to check task time and notes. In the proposed translation process model, monitoring manages and supervises the following six components:

- **Source text representation.** This process encompasses reading a source text part (e.g., a word, phrase, and a sentence) and interpreting its meaning in the source language. Source text interpretation is a prerequisite for the translator to be able to start searching for its target text equivalent. This representation process may occur subconsciously and synchronously during source text reading if the translator is familiar with its meaning in the source language; but it may take some time if the translator is unfamiliar with the meaning of the source text part being read, for example when it is jargon or has two potential source

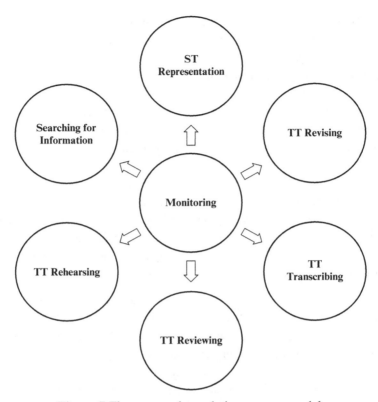

Figure 7 The proposed translation process model.

language meanings. In this latter case, the translator will reflect upon the meaning of the source text part, or – when necessary – use an online or printed reference to reach its optimal representation. Here, the monitor will interfere to approve or reject the translator's representation of the source text part. If rejected, another source text representation attempt will be made.

- **Searching for information.** According to the explanation given at the beginning of this subsection, the translator searches for different types of information during the translation task. It is expected that the translator will be preoccupied with searching for appropriate word/phrase equivalents. The translator normally starts with memory retrieval of the information stored in the mental lexicon; thus, memory retrieval draws upon long-term memory. If memory retrieval attempts have not succeeded, the translator searches for the target word/phrase equivalent in online or printed dictionaries or other lexical sources. The translator can also access machine translation and/or translation memory systems while performing tasks to facilitate their work. Meanwhile, they may follow the same memory retrieval/source use cycle in accessing other types of linguistic information; for example, when trying to phrase a particular sentence in an appropriate grammatical form, or when making sure of the meaning of a given word/phrase in the source language to represent it accurately. In each information search process, the monitor interferes again to approve or reject the information retrieved from the long-term memory or found in the sources consulted.

- **Target text rehearsing.** This process involves reformulating the target text before transcribing it. After retrieving the equivalent potentially matching the source text part, the translator mentally rehearses how to write it in a meaningful target text unit (e.g., a phrase, sentence part or a sentence). Target text rehearsing might be also made in a written form. The monitor normally supervises this process through accepting or rejecting the proposed target text alternative(s).
- **Target text reviewing.** As indicated in the beginning of this subsection, reviewing does not only include scanning or reading the transcribed target text, but it also encompasses checking the suitability of the proposed target text (e.g., through back translation or repeating the rehearsed text). After reviewing either the proposed target text or the transcribed one, the monitor decides upon the suitability of each alternative.
- **Target text transcribing.** This process involves transcribing the target text part for the first time through handwriting or typing tools. Once the target text part is transcribed, the monitor allows the translator to move to another process.
- **Target text revising.** Revision entails changing the transcribed target text as a result of identifying a problem in it. The revision process is triggered by the monitor and also ends once the revised target text part is approved by it. Translators' revisions can be classified into different categories such as the syntactic, lexical, morphological, content, and orthographic changes made (Englund Dimitrova 2005), the operation type (addition, deletion, and substitution), or the linguistic unit level changed (a sentence, a phrase or a word; grammar, spelling, or punctuation) (Abdel Latif 2021).

As the proposed translation process conceptualization shows, monitoring attends to each of the six remaining translation processes and the strategies representing them. It supervises these processes, evaluates the suitability of their outcomes, and based on this evaluation it allows the translator to move from one process to another. The monitor's supervisory role also interacts with the information retrieved from the long-term and short-term memories, the information found in the sources consulted, and with the source text translated so far and the target text produced. The translator performs a large number of cognitive activities; each activity relates to completing a part in the task.

A particular cognitive activity in the translation task is initiated by the monitor either through setting a goal for this activity or through noticing a problem. After the initiation of the translation activity by the monitor, the translator may engage in any other cognitive process such as source text representation, target text rehearsing or reviewing, or revision. The translator's cognitive processes occur recursively in no fixed order, and the one translation activity does not necessarily include all these processes; the occurrence of a particular set of translation processes in the one activity depends on activity purpose, time constraints, cognitive overload, or the automaticity resulting from the ease of the subtask at hand. For example, the cognitive overload associated with limited target language knowledge may cause the translator to be unable to monitor all the translation operations and to allocate more efforts to information search during the task (for an example in writing process research, see Abdel Latif (2014a)). The translator's cognitive style may also play an influential role in the implementation and regular use of particular translation processes. Likewise, a high degree of familiarity with the source text genre may lead the translator to rehearse target text parts less regularly or monitor some processes, or to undertake minimal information search during the task. The impact of source text genre and task familiarity on the automaticity of the translator's cognitive processes can be compared to the automaticity levels in car driving of novice drivers (who normally concentrate fully on their driving) versus expert drivers (who drive more automatically due to their driving familiarity and experience). Compare also this conscious–subconscious perspective to Oxford's (1990) view that language learners use cognitive strategies consciously at the beginning, but after some time they use them automatically. Despite the variance in using translation processes in different cognitive activities, the translator will use all of them while completing the whole translation task. In other words, varied attentional efforts will be allocated to different translation components and the strategies representing them depending primarily on the translator's target language proficiency, familiarity with source text genre, task complexity, and available information sources. These issues can be regarded as testable hypotheses in future research.

6 Conclusion

In this Element, the author has reviewed the developments in translation process research. The Element has specifically highlighted the key terms in translation process research, its data collection options, the developments it has witnessed over four decades, and the modelling efforts made in it so far. Besides, the work has proposed a translation process model which shows the role monitoring plays in managing and organizing translator cognition. Despite the developments made in translation process research during the past decades, it is still maturing. A decade ago, O'Brien (2015) reached a similar conclusion as she points out that this research area is still in its infancy, and views that 'there are many ways in which further development could take place by borrowing even more from more established disciplines' (p. 12). Arguably, writing process research is a more mature area that translation cognition studies may borrow from (see, e.g., Dam-Jensen and Heine (2013); Risku, Milosevic and Pein-Weber (2016)). Besides, psycholinguistics and cognitive psychology are two other related fields translation process research can benefit from.

Advancing translation process research and modelling requires addressing some methodological and contextual research gaps, and paying due attention to researching different translation process dimensions. Translation process research is more popular in academic environments within certain geographical regions rather than others. For example, it is mainly popular within Western European and South-East Asian universities, and, to a lesser extent, Southern-American ones. Therefore, more attention should be paid to investigating translators' processes in different international academic contexts. Such research could reveal important insights into how translators' cognitive processes may vary in different socio-cultural settings.

Methodologically, there is a need to make more use of introspective and retrospective data sources in translation process research. As shown in Section 3, translation process researchers have gradually abandoned the think-aloud method and concurrent verbalization data since the early 2010s. Because it may provide rich insights into translation processes, researchers should not abandon the think-aloud method; rather, its use and data analysis should be standardized. In addition, retrospective data sources are yet to be optimally and widely used in translation process studies. Such sources can be particularly useful in large-scale studies, as well as ethnographic studies conducted in translation workplaces. Combining think-aloud protocols with retrospective interviews could also help in reaching a better understanding of translators' cognitive processes.

Some translation process aspects remain unaddressed. One of these is translation fluency which can generally be defined as the ease of the translation process. While fluency has long been researched and been receiving increasing attention in writing process research (see, e.g., Abdel Latif 2009, 2013, 2014b; Matsuhashi 1981; Michel et al. 2020; Révész, Kourtali, & Mazgutova 2017; van Bruggen 1946), translation process fluency research is almost non-existent. In translation research, the term 'translation fluency' has occurred very infrequently, and it has been given some labels such as 'translation speed', and 'processing time'; that is, the speed of the translation process as measured by the processing time of text translation. (e.g., Qassem 2024; Rydning & Janyan 2008). Many volumes on translation cognition do not include even a single work on fluency (e.g., Alves & Jakobsen 2021; Hansen-Schirra, Czulo, & Hofmann 2017; Schwieter & Ferreira 2017; Shreve & Angelone 2010). Much research is also needed on other under-explored issues, such as translators' styles, translation revisions, and translation process training. Having a clearer picture of other dimensions of translation cognition – including effort allocation, information search, and target text rehearsing and reviewing – also requires further research. Such research should focus not only on profiling translators' processing of these text conversion dimensions but also on the explanatory factors accounting for their processing differences. Important also is exploring the insights we can obtain about such translation process components when using different data sources or data triangulation forms. Finally, we hardly know anything about collaborative translation processes. Therefore, attention should be paid to investigating the dynamics of group translation tasks using the dialogue think-aloud method in particular. With increasing research covering these issues and gaps, we will have a better understanding of the translation process.

References

Abdel Latif, M. M. M. 2008. A state-of-the-art review of the real-time computer-aided study of the writing process. *International Journal of English Studies* 8(1): 29–50.

Abdel Latif, M. M. M. 2009. Towards a new process-based indicator for measuring writing fluency: Evidence from L2 writers' think-aloud protocols. *Canadian Modern Language Review* 65(4): 531–558.

Abdel Latif, M. M. M. 2013. What do we mean by writing fluency and how can it be validly measured? *Applied Linguistics* 34(1): 99–105.

Abdel Latif, M. M. M. 2014a. Arab students' use of monitoring in their EFL composing: The role of linguistic knowledge. In K. M. Bailey and R. M. Damerow, eds., *The Teaching and Learning of English in the Arabic-speaking World*. New York: Routledge, pp. 32–47.

Abdel Latif, M. M. M. 2014b. Recent developments in EFL writing fluency measurement. In T. Muller, J. Adamson, P. Brown, and S. Herder, eds., *Exploring EFL Fluency in Asia*. London: Palgrave Macmillan, pp. 196–212.

Abdel Latif, M. M. M. 2018. Towards a typology of pedagogy-oriented translation and interpreting research. *The Interpreter and Translator Trainer* 12(3): 322–345.

Abdel Latif, M. M. M. 2019a. Using think-aloud protocols and interviews in investigating writers' composing processes: Combining concurrent and retrospective data. *International Journal of Research & Method in Education* 42(2): 111–123.

Abdel Latif, M. M. M. 2019b. Eye-tracking in recent L2 learner process research: A review of areas, issues, and methodological approaches. *System* 83: 25–35.

Abdel Latif, M. M. M. 2020. *Translator and Interpreter Education Research*. Cham: Springer.

Abdel Latif, M. M. M. 2021. Remodeling writers' composing processes: Implications for writing assessment. *Assessing Writing* 50: 1–16.

Alamargot, D., and Chanquoy, L. 2001. *Through the Models of Writing*. Amsterdam: Kluwer Academic, pp. 1–29.

Alves, F. 2005. Bridging the gap between declarative and procedural knowledge in the training of translators: Meta-reflection under scrutiny. *Meta* 50(4): 1–16.

Alves, F., and Campos, L. 2009. Translation technology in time: Investigating the impact of translation memory systems and time pressure on types of internal and external support. In A. L. Jakobsen, I. M. Mees, and S. Göpferich, eds.,

Behind the Mind: Methods, Models and Results in Translation Process Research. Frederiksberg: Samfundslitteratur Press, pp. 191–218.

Alves, F., and Hurtado Albir, A. 2010. Cognitive approaches. In Y. Gambier and L. van Doorslaer, eds., *Handbook of Translation Studies*. Amsterdam: John Benjamins, pp. 28–35.

Alves, F., and Hurtado Albir, A. 2017. Evolution, challenges, and perspectives for research on cognitive aspects of translation. In J. W. Schwieter and A. Ferreira, eds., *The Handbook of Translation and Cognition*. New Jersey: John Wiley & Sons, pp. 535–554.

Alves, F., and Jakobsen, A. L. 2021. *The Routledge Handbook of Translation and Cognition*. London: Routledge.

Alves, F., and Vale, C. 2011. On drafting and revision in translation: A corpus linguistics oriented analysis of translation process data. In S., Hansen-Schirra, S. Neumann, and O. Čulo, eds., *Annotation, Exploitation and Evaluation of Parallel Corpora*. Berlin: Language Science Press, pp. 105–122.

Alves, F., Pagano, A., and da Silva. I. A. 2009. A new window on translators' cognitive activity: Methodological issues in the combined use of eye tracking, key logging and retrospective protocols. In I. M. Mees, F. Alves, and S. Göpferich, eds., *Methodology, Technology and Innovation in Translation Process Research: A Tribute to Arnt Lykke Jakobsen*. Copenhagen: Samfundslitteratur, pp. 267–291.

Angelone, E. 2010a. Optimizing process-oriented translator training using freeware and FOSS screen recording applications. In P. Sandrini and M. García González, eds., *Translation and Openness*. Innsbruck: University of Innsbruck Press, pp. 131–143.

Angelone, E. 2010b. Uncertainty, uncertainty management and metacognitive problem solving in the translation task. In G. M. Shreve and E. Angelone, eds., *Translation and Cognition*. Amsterdam: John Benjamins, pp. 17–40.

Angelone, E. 2012. The place of screen recording in process-oriented translator training. *Rivista Internazionale di Tecnica della Traduzione* 14: 41–56.

Angelone, E. 2019. Process-oriented assessment of problems and errors in translation: Expanding horizons through screen recording. In E. Huertas-Barros, S. Vandepitte, and E. Iglesias-Fernandez, eds., *Quality Assurance and Assessment Practices in Translation and Interpreting*. Hershey: IGI Global, pp. 179–198.

Araghian, R., Ghonsooly, B., and Ghanizadeh, A. 2018. Investigating problem-solving strategies of translation trainees with high and low levels of self-efficacy. *Translation, Cognition & Behavior* 1(1): 74–97.

Asare, E. 2016. Ethnography of communication. In C. V. Angelelli and B. J. Baer, eds., *Researching Translation and Interpreting*. New York: Routledge, pp. 212–219.

Balling, L. W., Hvelplund, K. T., and Sjørup, A. C. 2014. Evidence of parallel processing during translation. *Meta* 59(2): 234–259.

Bardaji, A. G. 2009. Procedures, techniques, strategies: Translation process operators. *Perspectives: Studies in Translatology* 17(3): 161–173.

Bell, R. T. 1991. *Translation and Translating: Theory and Practice*. London: Longman.

Bernardini, S. 2001. Think-aloud protocols in translation research: Achievements, limits, future prospects. *Target: International Journal of Translation Studies* 13(2): 241–263.

Boehm, D. C. 1993. Mozartians, Beethovians, and the teaching of writing. *The Quarterly* 15(2): 15–18.

Borg, C. 2018. The phases of the translation process: Are they always three? *Conference Proceedings. Breaking Barriers*: 79–91.

Breedveld, H. 2002. Writing and revising processes in professional translation. *Across Languages and Cultures* 3(1): 91–100.

Bundgaard, K. 2017. Translator attitudes towards translator–computer interaction-findings from a workplace study. *Hermes: Journal of Language and Communication in Business* 56: 125–144.

Bundgaard, K., and Christensen, T. P. 2016. Translator–computer interaction in action: An observational process study of computer-aided translation. *Journal of Specialised Translation* 25: 106–130.

Bundgaard, K., and Christensen, T. P. 2019. Is the concordance feature the new black? A workplace study of translators' interaction with translation resources while post-editing TM and MT matches. *Journal of Specialised Translation* 31(31): 14–37.

Carl, M., and Dragsted, B. 2012. Inside the monitor model: Processes of default and challenged translation production. *TC3: Translation: Computation, Corpora, Cognition* 2(1): 127–145.

Carl, M., Dragsted, B., and Jakobsen, A. L. 2011. A taxonomy of human translation styles. *Translation Journal* 16(2): 155–168.

Chamot, A. U. 2001. The role of learning strategies in second language acquisition. In M. Breen, ed., *Learner Contribution to Language Learning: New Directions in Research*. Harlow: Longman, pp. 27–54.

Chandler, D. 1993. Writing strategies and writers' tools. *English Today* 9(2): 32–38.

Chenoweth, N. A., and Hayes, J. R. 2001. Fluency in writing: Generating texts in L1 and L2. *Written Communication* 18(1): 80–98.

Christensen, T. P. 2011. Studies on the mental processes in translation memory-assisted translation – The state of the art. *Trans-kom. ZeitschriftfürTranslationswissenschaft und Fachkommunikation* 4(2): 137–160.

Christensen, T. P., and Schjoldager, A. 2011. The impact of translation memory (TM) technology on cognitive processes: Student-translators' retrospective comments in an online questionnaire. In B. Sharp, M. Zock, M. Carl, and A. L. Jakobsen, eds., *Human-Machine Interaction in Translation*. Copenhagen: Samfundslitteratur, pp. 119–130.

Cohen, A. D. 1998. *Strategies in Learning and Using a Second Language*. London: Routledge .

Daems, J., Vandepitte, S., Hartsuiker, R. J., and Macken, L. 2017. Translation methods and experience: A comparative analysis of human translation and post-editing with students and professional translators. *Meta* 62(2): 245–270.

Dam-Jensen H., and Heine C. 2009. Process research methods and their application in the didactics of text production and translation. *Transkom* 2(1): 1–25.

Dam-Jensen, H., and Heine, C. 2013. Writing and translation process research: Bridging the gap (Introduction). *Journal of Writing Research* 5(1): 89–101.

Danks, H. J., and Griffin, J. 1997. Reading and translation: A psycholinguistic perspective. In H. J. Danks, G. M. Shreve, S. B. Fountain, and M. K. McBeath, eds., *Cognitive Processing in Translation and Interpreting*. Thousand Oaks: Sage, pp. 161–175.

Dechert, H. W., and Sandrock, U. 1986. Thinking-aloud protocols: The decomposition of language processing. In V. Cook, ed., *Experimental Approaches to Second Language Learning*. Oxford: Pergamon, pp. 111–126.

de Lima Fonseca, N. B. 2019. Analysing the impact of TAPs on temporal, technical and cognitive effort in monolingual post-editing. *Perspectives: Studies in Translation Theory and Practice* 27(4): 552–588.

Diamond, B. J., and Shreve, G. M. 2017. Deliberate practice and neurocognitive optimization of translation expertise. In J. W. Schwieter and A. Ferreira, eds., *The Handbook of Translation and Cognition*. New Jersey: John Wiley & Sons, pp. 476–495.

Dragsted, B. 2004. *Segmentation in Translation and Translation Memory Systems: An Empirical Investigation of Cognitive Segmentation and Effects of Integrating a TM System into the Translation Process*. PhD dissertation. (Copenhagen Working Papers in LSP 4.) Copenhagen: Samfundslitteratur.

Dragsted, B. 2006. Computer-aided translation as a distributed cognitive task. *Pragmatics & Cognition* 14(2): 443–464.

Dragsted, B. 2010. Co-ordination of reading and writing processes in translation: An eye on unchartered territory. In G. Shreve and E. Angelone, eds., *Translation and Cognition*. Amsterdam: John Benjamins, pp. 41–63.

Dragsted, B., and Carl, M. 2013. Towards a classification of translation styles based on eye-tracking and keylogging data. *Journal of Writing Research* 5(1): 133–158.

Dragsted, B., and Hansen, E. G. 2008. Comprehension and production in translation. In S. Göpferich, A. L. Jakobsen, and I. M. Mees, eds., *Looking at Eyes: Eye-Tracking Studies of Reading and Translation Processing.* Copenhagen: Samfundslitteratur, pp. 9–30.

Ehrensberger-Dow, M. 2014. Challenges of translation process research at the workplace. *MonTI* 7(2): 355–383.

Englund Dimitrova, B. 2005. *Expertise and Explicitation in the Translation Process.* Amsterdam: John Benjamins.

Englund Dimitrova, B., and Tiselius, E. 2009. Exploring retrospection as a research method for studying the translation process and the interpreting process. In I. M. Mees, F. Alves, and S. Göpferich, eds., *Methodology, Technology and Innovation in Translation Process Research: A Tribute to Arnt Lykke Jakobsen.* Copenhagen: Samfundslitteratur, pp. 109–134.

Englund Dimitrova, B., and Tiselius, E. 2014. Retrospection in interpreting and translation: Explaining the process? *MonTI* 1: 177–200.

Ericsson, K., and Simon, H. 1980. Verbal reports as data. *Psychological Review* 87(3): 215–251.

Ericsson, K. A., and Simon, H. A. 1993. *Protocol Analysis: Verbal Reports as Data.* Cambridge: MIT Press.

Faber, D., and Hjort-Pedersen, M. 2009. Manifestations of inference processes in legal translation. In A. L. Jakobsen, I. M. Mees, and S. Göpferich, eds., *Behind the Mind: Methods, Models and Results in Translation Process Research.* Frederiksberg: Samfundslitteratur Press, pp. 107–124.

Faigley, L., Cherry, R. D., Jolliffe, D. A., and Skinner, A. 1985. *Assessing Writers' Knowledge and Processes of Composing.* New Jersey: Ablex.

Flower, L., and Hayes, J. R. 1977. Problem-solving strategies and the writing process. *College English* 39(4): 449–461.

Flower, L., and Hayes, J. R. 1980. The cognition of discovery: Defining a rhetorical problem. *College Composition and Communication* 31(1): 21–32.

Flower, L., and Hayes, J. R. 1981. A cognitive process theory of writing. *College Composition & Communication* 32(4): 365–387.

Gallego-Hernández, D. 2015. The use of corpora as translation resources: A study based on a survey of Spanish professional translators. *Perspectives: Studies in Translation Theory and Practice* 23(3): 375–391.

Gerloff, P. 1986. Second language learners' reports on the interpretive process: Talkaloud protocols of translation. In J. House and S. Blum-Kulka, eds.,

Interlingual and Intercultural Communication: Discourse and Cognition in Translation. Tübingen: Gunter Narr, pp. 243–262.

Gerloff, P. 1987. Identifying the unit of analysis in translation: Some uses of think-aloud protocol data. In C. Færch and G. Kasper, eds., *Introspection in Second Language Research.* Philadelphia: Multilingual Matters, pp. 135–158.

Gerloff, P. 1988. *From French to English: A Look at the Translation Process in Students, Bilinguals, and Professional Translators.* PhD dissertation, Harvard University, USA.

Gile, D. 2004. Integrated problem and decision reporting as a translator training tool. *The Journal of Specialised Translation* 2(2): 2–20.

Gile, D. 2009. *Basic Concepts and Models for Interpreter and Translator Training* Amsterdam: John Benjamins.

Gile, D., and Lei, V. 2020. Translation, effort and cognition. In F. Alves and A. L. Jakobsen, eds., *The Routledge Handbook of Translation and Cognition.* London: Routledge, pp. 263–278.

Göpferich, S. 2009. Towards a model of translation competence and its acquisition: The longitudinal study TransComp. In A. L. Jakobsen, I. M. Mees, and S. Göpferich, eds., *Behind the Mind: Methods, Models and Results in Translation Process Research.* Frederiksberg: Samfundslitteratur Press, pp. 11–37.

Göpferich, S., and Jääskeläinen, R. 2009. Process research into the development of translation competence: Where are we, and where do we need to go? *Across Languages and Cultures* 10(2): 169–191.

Göpferich, S., and Nelezen, B. 2014. The language-(in) dependence of writing skills: Translation as a tool in writing process research and writing instruction. *MonTI. Monografías de traducción e interpretación* 1: 117–149.

Göpferich, S., Jakobsen, A. L., and Mees, I. M. 2008. *Looking at Eyes: Eye-tracking Studies of Reading and Translation Processing.* Copenhagen: Samfundslitteratur.

Green, A. 1998. *Verbal Protocol Analysis in Language Testing Research: A Handbook. Studies in Language Testing.* Cambridge: Cambridge University Press.

Greene, S., and Higgins, L. 1994. Once upon a time: The use of retrospective accounts in building theory in composition. In P. Smagorinsky, ed., *Speaking about Writing: Reflections on Research Methodology.* London: SAGE, pp. 115–140.

Guerberof Arenas, A. 2013. What do professional translators think about post-editing. *The Journal of Specialised Translation* 19: 75–95.

Hansen, G. 2003. Controlling the process: Theoretical and methodological reflections on research into translation processes. In F. Alves, ed., *Triangulation*

Translation: Perspectives in Process Oriented Research. Amsterdam: John Benjamins, pp. 25–42.

Hansen, G. 2005. Experience and emotion in empirical translation research with think-aloud and retrospection. *Meta* 50(2): 511–521.

Hansen, G. 2006. Retrospection methods in translator training and translation research. *Journal of Specialized Translation* 5(1): 2–41.

Hansen-Schirra, S., Czulo, O., and Hofmann, S. 2017. *Empirical Modelling of Translation and Interpreting*. Belin: Language Science Press.

Hayes, J. R., and Flower, L. 1980. Identifying the organization of writing processes. In L. Gregg and E. R. Steinberg, eds., *Cognitive Processes in Writing*. Hillsdale: Lawrence Erlbaum, pp. 3–30.

Heeb, A. H. 2016. Professional translators' self-concepts and directionality: Indications from translation process research. *The Journal of Specialised Translation* 25: 74–88.

Hillocks, G. 1986. *Research on Written Composition*. Urbana: ERIC Clearinghouse on Reading and Communication Skills.

Hirci, N. 2012. Electronic reference resources for translators: Implications for productivity and translation quality. *The Interpreter and Translator Trainer* 6(2): 219–236.

Hirvonen, M. I., and Tiittula, L. M. 2018. How are translations created? Using multimodal conversation analysis to study a team translation process. *Linguistica Antverpiensia, New Series: Themes in Translation Studies* 17: 157–173.

House, J. 1988. Talking to oneself or thinking with others? On using different thinking-aloud methods in translation. *Fremdsprachen lehren und lernen* 17: 84–99.

Hurtado Albir, A. H., and Alves, F. 2009. Translation as a cognitive activity. In J. Munday, ed., *The Routledge Companion to Translation Studies*. London: Routledge, pp. 54–73.

Hvelplund, K. T. 2011. *Allocation of Cognitive Resources in Translation: An Eye-Tracking and Key-Logging Study*. PhD thesis, Copenhagen Business School.

Hvelplund, K. T. 2014. Eye tracking and the translation process: Reflections on the analysis and interpretation of eye-tracking data. *MonTI. Monografías de Traducción e Interpretación* 1: 201–223.

Hvelplund, K. T. 2017. Four fundamental types of reading during translation. In A. L. Jakobsen and B. Mesa-Lao, eds., *Translation in Transition: Between Cognition, Computing and Technology*. Amsterdam: John Benjamins, pp. 55–77.

Hvelplund, K. T. 2019. Digital resources in the translation process-attention, cognitive effort and processing flow. *Perspectives: Studies in Translation Theory and Practice* 27(4): 510–524.

Hvelplund, K. T. 2023. Institutional translation and the translation process. In T. Svoboda, Ł. Biel, and V. Sosoni, eds., *Institutional Translator Training*. London: Routledge, pp. 92–110.

Hwang, M., and Lee, H. 2017. Development and validation of the English writing strategy inventory. *System* 68: 60–71.

Immonen, S. 2006. Translation as a writing process: Pauses in translation versus monolingual text production. *Target: International Journal of Translation Studies* 18(2): 313–336.

Jääskeläinen, R. 1987. *What Happens in a Translation Process: Think-Aloud Protocols of Translation*. Unpublished Pro gradu Thesis. Savonlinna School of Translation Studies, University of Joensuu.

Jääskeläinen, R. 1989. Translation assignment in professional vs. non-professional translation: A think-aloud protocol study. In C. Séguinot, ed., *The Translation Process*. Toronto: H. G. Publications, pp. 87–98.

Jääskeläinen, R. 1999. *Tapping the Process: An Explorative Study of the Cognitive and Affective Factors Involved in Translating*. Joensuu: University of Joensuu.

Jääskeläinen, R. 2000. Focus on methodology in think-aloud studies on translating. In S. Tirkkonen-Condit and R. Jääskeläinen, eds., *Tapping and Mapping the Processes of Translation and Interpreting: Outlooks on Empirical Research*. Amsterdam: John Benjamins, pp. 71–82.

Jääskeläinen, R. 2002. Think-aloud protocol studies into translation: An annotated bibliography. *Target: International Journal of Translation Studies* 14(1): 107–136.

Jakobsen, A. L. 1999. Logging target text production with Translog. In G. Hansen, ed, *Probing the Process in Translation: Methods and Results*. Copenhagen: Samfundslitteratur, pp. 9–20.

Jakobsen, A. L. 2002. Orientation, segmentation, and revision in translation. In G. Hansen, ed., *Empirical Translation Studies: Process and Product*. Copenhagen: Samfundslitteratur, pp. 191–204.

Jakobsen, A. L. 2003. Effects of think aloud on translation speed, revision, and segmentation. In F. Alves, ed., *Triangulating Translation: Perspectives in Process-oriented Research*. Amsterdam: John Benjamins, pp. 69–95.

Jakobsen, A. L. 2011. Tracking translators' keystrokes and eye movements with Translog. In C. Alvstad, E. Tiselius, and A. Hild, eds., *Methods and Strategies of Process Research*. Amsterdam: John Benjamins, pp. 37–55.

Jakobsen, A. L. 2017. Translation process research. In J. W. Schwieter and A. Ferreira, eds., *The Handbook of Translation and Cognition*. New Jersey: John Wiley & Sons, pp. 19–49.

Jakobsen, A. L. 2018. Moving translation, revision, and post-editing boundaries. In H. V. Dam, M. N. Brøgger, and K. K. Zethsen, eds., *Moving Boundaries in Translation Studies*. London: Routledge, pp. 64–80.

Jakobsen, A. L., and Jensen, K. T. H. 2008. Eye movement behaviour across four different types of reading task. In S. Gopferich, A. L. Jakobsen, and I. M. Mees, eds., *Looking at Eyes: Eye-tracking Studies of Reading and Translation Processing*. Copenhagen: Samfundslitteratur, pp. 103–124.

Jakobsen, A. L., and Schou, L. 1999. Translog documentation. In G. Hansen, ed., *Probing the Process in Translation: Methods and Results*. Copenhagen Studies in Language 24, Copenhagen: Samfundslitteratur, pp. 151–186.

Jia, Y., Carl, M., and Wang, X. 2019. How does the post-editing of neural machine translation compare with from-scratch translation? A product and process study. *The Journal of Specialised Translation* 31(1): 60–86.

Just, M. A., and Carpenter, P. A. 1980. A theory of reading: From eye fixations to comprehension. *Psychological Review* 87(4): 329–354.

Kellogg, R. 1996. A model of working memory in writing. In M. Levy and S. Ransdell, eds., *The Science of Writing: Theories, Methods, Individual Differences, and Applications*. Hillsdale: Lawrence Erlbaum Associates, pp. 57–71.

Kim, R. 2006. Use of extralinguistic knowledge in translation. *Meta* 51(2): 284–303.

Kiraly, D. C. 1995. *Pathways to Translation: Pedagogy and Process*. Kent: Kent State University Press.

Kobayashi, H., and Rinnert, C. 1992. Effects of first language on second language writing: Translation versus direct composition. *Language Learning* 42(2): 183–209.

Koglin, A., and Cunha, R. 2019. Investigating the post-editing effort associated with machinetranslated metaphors: A process-driven analysis. *The Journal of Specialised Translation* 31: 38–59.

Königs, F. G. 1986. Der Vorgang des Übersetzens: Theoretische Modelle und praktischer Vollzug. Zum Verhältnis von Theorie und Praxis in der Übersetzungswissenschaft. *Lebende Sprachen* 1(1): 5–12.

Königs, F. G. 1987. Was beim Übersetzen passiert. Theoretische Aspekte, empirische Befunde und praktische Konsequenzen. *Die neueren Sprachen* 86(2): 162–185.

Krings, H. P. 1986. Translation problems and translation strategies of advanced German learners of French (L2). In J. House and S. Blum-Kulka, eds.,

Interlingual and Intercultural Communication. Tubingen: Gunter Narr, pp. 263–275.

Krings, H. P. 1987. The use of introspective data in translation. In C. Faerch and G. Kasper, eds., *Introspection in Second-Language Research*. Clevedon: Multilingual Matters, pp. 159–175.

Krings, H. P. 1988. Blick in die 'black box' – Eine Fallstudie zum Übersetzung-sprozess bei Berufsübersetzern. In R. Arntz, ed., *Textlinguistik und Fachsprache*. Hildesheim: Olms, pp. 393–412.

Krings, H. P. 2001. *Repairing Texts: Empirical Investigations of Machine Translation Post-editing Processes*. Kent: Kent State University Press.

Kruger, H. 2016. What's happening when nothing's happening? Combining eyetracking and keylogging to explore cognitive processing during pauses in translation production. *Across Languages and Cultures* 17(1): 25–52.

Kumpulainen, M. 2015. On the operationalisation of 'pauses' in translation process research. *Translation & Interpreting* 7(1): 47–58.

Kussmaul, P. 1997. Comprehension processes and translation. A think-aloud protocol (TAP) study. In M. Snell-Hornby, Z. Jettmarová, and K. Kaindl, eds., *Translation as Intercultural Communication: Selected Papers from the EST Congress, Prague 1995*. Amsterdam: John Benjamins, pp. 239–248.

Kussmaul, P., and Tirkkonen-Condit, S. 1995. Think-aloud protocol analysis in translation studies. *TTR: Traduction, terminologie, rédaction* 8(1): 177–199.

Kuznik, A., and Olalla-Soler, C. 2018. Results of PACTE Group's experimental research on translation competence acquisition. The acquisition of the instrumental sub-competence. *Across Languages and Cultures* 19(1): 19–51.

Kvėdytė, V., and Baranauskienė, R. 2005. Translation strategies in the process of translation: A Psycholinguistic investigation. *Journal of Young Scientists* 3(7): 189–195.

Lauffer, S. 2002. The translation process: An analysis of observational methodology. *Cadernos de traduçao* 2(10): 59–74.

LeBlanc, M. 2013. Translators on translation memory (TM): Results of an ethnographic study in three translation services and agencies. *Translation & Interpreting* 5(2): 1–13.

Leow, R. P., and Morgan-Short, K. 2004. To think aloud or not to think aloud: The issue of reactivity in SLA research methodology. *Studies in Second Language Acquisition* 26(1): 35–57.

Levelt, W. J. M. 1999. Producing spoken language: A blueprint of the speaker. In C. M. Brown and P. Hagoort, eds., *The Neurocognition of Language*. New York: Oxford University Press, pp. 83–122.

Levý, J. 1967. Translation as a decision process. In P. Friedrich, ed., *To Honour Román Jakobson: Essays on the Occasion of His Seventieth Birthday.* Mouton: The Hague, pp. 1171–1182.

Levy, C. M., and Ransdell, S. E. 1996. Writing signatures. In C. M. Levy and S. E. Ransdel, eds., *The Science of Writing: Theories, Methods, Individual Differences and Applications.* Mahwah: Lawrence Erlbaum Associates, pp. 149–161.

Li, D. 2004. Trustworthiness of think-aloud protocols in the study of translation processes. *International Journal of Applied Linguistics* 14(3): 301–313.

Li, D., and Cheng, M. 2011. Monologue vs. dialogue verbal reporting: Research subjects' perceptions. *Journal of Translation Studies* 10(1): 43–56.

Li, D., Lei, V., and He, Y. 2019. *Researching Cognitive Processes of Translation.* Cham: Springer.

Lörscher, W. 1991. *Translation Performance, Translation Process, and Translation Strategies: A Psycholinguistic Investigation.* Tübingen: Gunter Narr.

Lörscher, W. 1992. Investigating the translation process. *Meta* 37(3): 426–439.

Lörscher, W. 2002. A model for the analysis of translation processes within a framework of systemic linguistics. *Cadernos de Tradução* 2(10): 97–112.

Lörscher, W. 2005. The translation process: Methods and problems of its investigation. *Meta* 50(2): 597–608.

Massey, G., and Ehrensberger-Dow, M. 2011. Commenting on translation: Implications for translator training. *The Journal of Specialised Translation* 16: 26–41.

Massey, G., and Ehrensberger-Dow, M. 2013. Evaluating translation processes: Opportunities and challenges. In D. C. Kiraly, S. Hansen, and K. Maksymski, eds., *New Prospects and Perspectives for Educating Language Mediators.* Tübingen: Gunter Narr, pp. 157–180.

Matrat, C. M. 1992. *Investigating the Translation Process: Thinking-aloud Versus Joint Activity.* Unpublished PhD thesis, University of Delaware.

Matsuhashi, A. 1981. Pausing and planning: The tempo of written discourse production. *Research in the Teaching of English* 15(2): 113–134.

Matsumoto, K. 1994. Introspection, verbal reports and second language learning strategy research. *The Canadian Modern Language Review* 50(2): 363–385.

Michel, M., Révész, A., Lu, X. et al. 2020. Investigating L2 writing processes across independent and integrated tasks: A mixed-methods study. *Second Language Research* 36(3): 307–334.

Mizowaki, T., Ogawa, H., and Yamada, M. 2023. Linear vs. non-linear translation in parallel text reading. *Ampersand* 10: 100124, 1–9.

Mondahl, M., and Jensen, K. A. 1996. Lexical search strategies in translation. *Meta* 41(1): 97–113.

Mossop, B. 2000. The workplace procedures of professional translators. In A. Chesterman, N. G. San Salvador, and Y. Gambier, eds., *Translation in Context*. Amsterdam: John Benjamins, pp. 39–48.

Muñoz Martín, R. 2009. Expertise and environment in translation. *Mutatis Mutandis: Revista Latinoamericana de Traducción* 2(1): 24–37.

Muñoz Martín, R. 2010a. On paradigms and cognitive translatology. In G. Shreve and E. Angelone, eds., *Translation and Cognition*. Amsterdam: John Benjamins, pp. 169–187.

Muñoz Martín, R. 2010b. Leave no stone unturned: On the development of cognitive translatology. *Translation & Interpreting Studies* 5(2): 145–162.

Muñoz Martín, R. 2016. Processes of what models? On the cognitive indivisibility of translation acts and events. *Translation Spaces* 5(1): 145–161.

Muñoz Martín, R., and Cardona Guerra, J. M. 2019. Translating in fits and starts: Pause thresholds and roles in the research of translation processes. *Perspectives: Studies in Translation Theory and Practice* 27(4): 525–551.

Muñoz Martín, R., and Olalla-Soler, C. 2022. Translating is not (only) problem-solving. *The Journal of Specialised Translation* 38: 3–31.

Neubert, A. 1997. Postulates for a theory of translation. In J. M. Danks, G. M. Shreve, S. B. Fountain, and M. K. McBeath, eds., *Cognitive Processes in Translation and Interpreting*. Thousand Oaks: Sage, pp. 1–24.

Nunes Vieira, L. 2017. Cognitive effort and different task foci in post-editing of machine translation: A think-aloud study. *Across Languages and Cultures* 18(1): 79–105.

Núñez, J. L., and Bolaños-Medina, A. 2018. Predictors of problem-solving in translation: Implications for translator training. *The Interpreter and Translator Trainer* 12(3): 282–298.

O'Brien, S. 2006a. Pauses as indicators of cognitive effort in post-editing machine translation output. *Across Languages and Cultures* 7(1): 1–21.

O'Brien, S. 2006b. Eye-tracking and translation memory matches. *Perspectives: Studies in Translation Theory and Practice* 14(3): 185–205.

O'Brien, S. 2007. Eye-tracking and translation memory matches. *Perspectives: Studies in Translation Theory and Practice* 14(3): 185–205.

O'Brien, S. 2008. Processing fuzzy matches in translation memory tools: An eye-tracking analysis. *Copenhagen Studies in Language* 36: 79–102.

O'Brien, S. 2009. Eye tracking in translation process research: Methodological challenges and solutions. In I. M. Mees, F. Alves, and S. Göpferich, eds., *Methodology, Technology and Innovation in Translation Process Research: A Tribute to Arnt Lykke Jakobsen*. Copenhagen: Samfundslitteratur, pp. 251–266.

O'Brien, S. 2015. The borrowers: Researching the cognitive aspects of translation. In M. Ehrensberger-Dow, S. Göpferich, and S. O'Brien, eds., *Interdisciplinarity in Translation and Interpreting Process Research*. Amsterdam: John Benjamins, pp. 5–17.

O'Brien, S., O'Hagan, M., and Flanagan, M. 2010. Keeping an eye on the UI design of translation memory: How do translators use the 'concordance' feature? *European Conference on Cognitive Ergonomics*, Delft, 1–4.

Oster, K. 2017. The influence of self-monitoring on the translation of cognates. In S. Hansen- Schirra, O. Czulo, and S. Hofmann, eds., *Empirical Modelling of Translation and Interpreting*. Berlin: Language Science Press, pp. 23–39.

Oxford, R. 1990. *Language Learning Strategies: What Every Teacher Should Know*. New York: Newbury House.

Oxford, R. L., and Burry-Stock, J. A. 1995. Assessing the use of language learning strategies worldwide with ESL/EFL version of the Strategy Inventory for Language Learning (SILL). *System* 23(1): 1–23.

PACTE. 2000. Acquiring translation competence: Hypotheses and methodological problems of a research project. In A. Beeby, D. Ensinger, and M. Presas, eds., *Investigating Translation: Selected Papers from the 4th International Congress on Translation, Barcelona, 1998*. Amsterdam: John Benjamins, pp. 99–106.

PACTE. 2003. Building a translation competence model. In F. Alves, ed., *Triangulating Translation: Perspectives in Process-oriented Research*. Amsterdam: John Benjamins, pp. 43–66.

PACTE. 2005. Investigating translation competence: Conceptual and methodological issues. *Meta* 50(2): 609–619.

PACTE. 2019. Evolution of the efficacy of the translation process in translation competence acquisition. *Meta* 64(1): 242–265.

Pavlović, N. 2007. *Directionality in Collaborative Translation Processes: A Study of Novice Translators*. PhD dissertation, Universitat Rovira i Virgili, Spain, University of Zagreb, Croatia.

Pavlović, N. 2009. More ways to explore the translating mind: Collaborative translation protocols. In A. L. Jakobsen, I. M. Mees, and S. Göpferich, eds., *Behind the Mind: Methods, Models and Results in Translation Process Research*. Frederiksberg: Samfundslitteratur Press, pp. 81–105.

Pavlović, N., and Jensen, K. 2009. Eye tracking translation directionality. *Translation Research Projects* 2: 93–109.

Perl, S. 1979. The composing processes of unskilled college writers. *Research in the Teaching of English* 13(4): 317–336.

Petrić, B., and Czárl, B. 2003. Validating a writing strategy questionnaire. *System* 31(2): 187–215.

Pym, A. 2009. Using process studies in translator training: Self-discovery through lousy experiments. In I. M. Mees, F. Alves, and S. Göpferich, eds., *Methodology, Technology and Innovation in Translation Process Research: A Tribute to Arnt Lykke Jakobsen*. Copenhagen: Samfundslitteratur, pp. 135–156.

Pym, A. 2011. Translator training. In K. Malmkjær and K. Windle, eds., *The Oxford Handbook of Translation Studies*. Oxford: Oxford University Press, pp. 314–321.

Qassem, M. 2024. Adequacy, fluency and cognitive processes: Evidence from translating English news articles into Arabic. *Interactive Learning Environment* 5: 1–16.

Révész, A., Kourtali, N.-E., and Mazgutova, D. 2017. Effects of task complexity on L2 writing behaviours and linguistic complexity. *Language Learning* 67(1): 208–241.

Rijlaarsdam, G., and van den Bergh, H. 1996. The dynamics of composing: An agenda for research into an interactive model of writing: Many questions, some answers. In C. M. Levy and S. Ransdell, eds., *The Science of Writing: Theories, Methods, Individual Differences, and Applications*. Mahwah: Lawrence Erlbaum, pp. 107–125.

Risku, H. 2014. Translation process research as interaction research: From mental to socio-cognitive processes. *MonTI. Monografías de Traducción e Interpretación* 1: 331–353.

Risku, H. 2017. Ethnographies of translation and situated cognition. In J. W. Schwieter and A. Ferreira, eds., *The Handbook of Translation and Cognition*. New Jersey: John Wiley & Sons, pp. 290–310.

Risku, H., Milosevic, J., and Pein-Weber, C. 2016. *Writing vs. Translating*. Amsterdam: John Benjamins.

Robert, I. S. 2013. Translation revision: Does the revision procedure matter? In C. Way, S. Vandepitte, R. Meylaerts, and M. Bartłomiejczyk, eds., *Treks and Tracks in Translation Studies*. Amsterdam: John Benjamins, pp. 87–102.

Robert, I. S. 2014. Investigating the problem-solving strategies of revisers through triangulation. An exploratory study. *Translation and Interpreting Studies* 9(1): 88–108.

Robert, I. S., and Brunette, L. 2016. Should revision trainees think aloud while revising somebody else's translation? Insights from an empirical study with professionals. *Meta* 61(2): 320–345.

Robert, I. S., and van Waes, L. 2014. Selecting a translation revision procedure: Do common sense and statistics agree? *Perspectives: Studies in Translation Theory and Practice* 22(3): 304–320.

Roca de Larios, J., Manchón, R. M., and Murphy, L. 2008. The foreign language writer's strategic behaviour in the allocation of time to writing processes. *Journal of Second Language Writing* 17(1): 30–47.

Roca de Larios, J., Murphy, L., and Manchon, R. 1999. The use of restructuring strategies in EFL writing: A study of Spanish learners of English as a foreign language. *Journal of Second Language Writing* 8(1): 13–44.

Ruiz-Funes, M. 1999. The process of reading-to-write used by a skilled Spanish-as-a-foreign language student: A case study. *Foreign Language Annals* 32(1): 45–62.

Russo, J. E., Johnson, E. J., and Stephens, D. L. 1989. The validity of verbal protocols. *Memory & Cognition* 17: 759–769.

Rydning, A. F., and Janyan, A. 2008. Eye movement recordings as a tool for studying mental simulation of speed in text processing by professional translators. *Forum: International Journal of Interpretation and Translation* 6(1): 59–74.

Schaeffer, M. J., and Carl, M. 2013. Shared representations and the translation process: A recursive model. *Translation & Interpreting Studies* 8(2): 169–190.

Schaeffer, M., Nitzke, J., Tardel, A. et al. 2019. Eye-tracking revision processes of translation students and professional translators. *Perspectives: Studies in Translation Theory and Practice* 27(4): 589–603.

Schaeffer, M. J., Paterson, K., McGowan, V. A., White, S. J., and Malmkjær, K. 2017. Reading for Translation. In A. L. Jakobsen and B. Mesa-Lao, eds., *Translation in Transition: Between Cognition, Computing and Technology.* Amsterdam: John Benjamins, pp. 18–54.

Schmid, A. 1994. Gruppenprotokolle- ein Einblick in die black box des Übersetzens. *TexTconTexT* 9: 121–146.

Séguinot, C. 1989. The translation process: An experimental study. In Séguinot, ed., *The Translation Process.* Toronto: H. G. Publications, pp. 21–53.

Sharmin, S., Špakov, O., Räihä, K., and Jakobsen, A. L. 2008. Where on the screen do translation students look while translating, and for how long? In S. Göpferich, A. L. Jakobsen, and I. M. Mees, eds., *Looking at Eyes: Eye-Tracking Studies of Reading and Translation Processing.* Copenhagen: Samfundslitteratur, pp. 31–51 .

Shih, C. Y. 2006. Revision from translators' point of view: An interview study. *Target: International Journal of Translation Studies* 18(2): 295–312.

Shih, C. Y. Y. 2015. Problem-solving and decision-making in translation revision: Two case studies. *Across Languages and Cultures* 16(1): 69–92.

Shreve, G. M. and Angelone, E. 2010. *Translation and Cognition.* Amsterdam: John Benjamins.

Shreve, G. M., and Koby, G. S. 1997. Introduction: What's in the 'black box'? Cognitive science and translation studies. In J. H., Danks, G. M. Shreve, S. B., Fountain, and M. M. M. Mcbeath, eds., *Cognitive Process in Translation and Interpreting*. London: SAGE, pp. xi–xviii.

Shreve, G. M., Schäffner, C., Danks, J. H., and Griffin, J. 1993. Is there a special kind of 'reading' for translation? An empirical investigation of reading in the translation process. *Target: International Journal of Translation Studies* 5(1): 21–41.

Smagorinsky, P. 1994. *Speaking about Writing: Reflections on Research Methodology*. Thousand Oaks: SAGE.

Sun, S. 2011. Think-aloud-based translation process research: Some methodological considerations. *Meta* 56(4): 928–951.

Sun, S. 2019. Measuring difficulty in translation and post-editing: A review. In D. Li, V. Lei, and Y. He, eds., *Researching Cognitive Processes of Translation*. Cham: Springer, pp. 139–168.

Sun, S., Li, T., and Zhou, X. 2020. Effects of thinking aloud on cognitive effort in translation. *Linguistica Antverpiensia, New Series: Themes in Translation Studies* 19: 132–151.

Sycz-Opoń, J. 2019. Information-seeking behaviour of translation students at the University of Silesia during legal translation–an empirical investigation. *The Interpreter and Translator Trainer* 13(2): 152–176.

Temizöz, Ö. 2013. *Postediting Machine Translation Output and Its Revision: Subject-Matter Experts versus Professional Translators*. Doctoral dissertation, Universitat Rovira i Virgili.

Tirkkonen-Condit, S. 1987. A pilot study of an aspect of the translation process. *Neuphilologische Mitteilungen* 88: 221–229.

Tirkkonen-Condit, S. 1989. Professional vs. non-professional translation: A think-aloud protocol study. In C. Séguinot, ed., *The Translation Process*. Toronto: H.G. Publications, pp. 73–85.

Tirkkonen-Condit, S. 2005. The monitor model revisited: Evidence from process research. *Meta* 50(2): 405–414.

Uzawa, K. 1996. Second language learners' processes of L1 writing, L2 writing, and translation from L1 into L2. *Journal of Second Language Writing* 5(3): 271–294.

van Bruggen, J. A. 1946. Factors affecting regularity of the flow of words during written composition. *Journal of Experimental Education* 15(2): 133–155.

van Waes, L., and Schellens, P. J. 2003. Writing profiles: The effect of the writing mode on pausing and revision patterns of experienced writers. *Journal of Pragmatics* 35(6): 829–853.

Vinay, J. P., and Darbelnet, J. 1958. *Stylistique cosparele du frangals et de l'anglais*. Paris: Didier.

Vottonen, E., and Kujamäki, M. 2021. On what grounds? Justifications of student translators for their translation solutions. *The Interpreter and Translator Trainer* 15(3): 306–325.

Wilss, W. 1994. A framework for decision-making in translation. *Target: International Journal of Translation Studies* 6(2): 131–150.

Wilss, W. 1996. *Knowledge and Skills in Translator Behaviour*. Amsterdam: John Benjamins.

Xiao, K., and Halverson, S. L. 2021. Cognitive Translation and Interpreting Studies (CTIS): Emerging trends in epistemology and methodology. *Cognitive Linguistic Studies* 8(2): 235–250.

Yang, C., Hu, G., and Zhang, L. J. 2014. Reactivity of concurrent verbal reporting in second language writing. *Journal of Second Language Writing* 24: 51–70.

Yang, C., Wang, Y., and Fan, N. 2022. Are parallel translation tasks parallel in difficulty? An eye-tracking study. *Perspectives: Studies in Translation Theory and Practice* 30(4): 711–726.

Yu, G., He, L., and Isaacs, T. 2017. *The Cognitive Processes of Taking IELTS Academic Writing Task One: An Eye-Tracking Study*. The British Council.

Zhang, L. J., and Qin, T. L. 2018. Validating a questionnaire on EFL writers' metacognitive awareness of writing strategies in multimedia environments. In A. Haukås, C. Bjørke, and M. Dypedahl, eds., *Metacognition in Language Learning and Teaching*. London: Routledge, pp. 157–178.

Acknowledgements

I would like to gratefully thank Professor Kirsten Malmkjær (the Series Editor) and the two anonymous reviewers for their insightful comments and suggestions which helped in improving the content quality of this work.

About the Author

Muhammad M. M. Abdel Latif is an associate professor of English language education at the Faculty of Graduate Studies of Education. Cairo University, Egypt. He has published research papers in more than twenty internationally well-known and ranked journals. He is also the author of *Translator and Interpreter Education Research: Areas, Methods and Trends* (published by Springer). ORCID: https://orcid.org/0000-0003-4002-822X

Cambridge Elements ☰

Translation and Interpreting

The series is edited by Kirsten Malmkjær with Sabine Braun as associate editor for Elements focusing on Interpreting.

Kirsten Malmkjær
University of Leicester

Kirsten Malmkjær is Professor Emeritus of Translation Studies at the University of Leicester. She has taught Translation Studies at the universities of Birmingham, Cambridge, Middlesex and Leicester and has written extensively on aspects of both the theory and practice of the discipline. *Translation and Creativity* (London: Routledge) was published in 2020 and *The Cambridge Handbook of Translation*, which she edited, was published in 2022. She is preparing a volume entitled *Introducing Translation* for the Cambridge Introductions to Language and Linguistics series.

Editorial Board

About the Series

Elements in Translation and Interpreting present cutting edge studies on the theory, practice and pedagogy of translation and interpreting. The series also features work on machine learning and AI, and human-machine interaction, exploring how they relate to multilingual societies with varying communication and accessibility needs, as well as text-focused research.

Cambridge Elements ≡

Translation and Interpreting

Elements in the Series

A full series listing is available at: www.cambridge.org/EITI

Printed in the United States
by Baker & Taylor Publisher Services